The
Principal's
Guide to
Managing
Communication

 **Leadership for Learning**

Series Editors
Willis D. Hawley and E. Joseph Schneider

Joseph Murphy
Leadership for Literacy: Research-Based Practice, PreK–3

P. Karen Murphy, Patricia A. Alexander
Understanding How Students Learn: A Guide for Instructional Leaders

E. Joseph Schneider, Lara L. Hollenczer
The Principal's Guide to Managing Communication

Please call our toll-free number (800-818-7243)
or visit our website (www.corwinpress.com)
to order individual titles or the entire series.

The
Principal's
Guide to
Managing
Communication

E. Joseph Schneider
Lara L. Hollenczer

Corwin Press
A SAGE Publications Company
Thousand Oaks, California

For information:

Corwin Press
A Sage Publications Company
2455 Teller Road
Thousand Oaks, California 91320
www.corwinpress.com

Sage Publications Ltd.
1 Oliver's Yard
55 City Road
London EC1Y 1SP
United Kingdom

Sage Publications India Pvt. Ltd.
B-42, Panchsheel Enclave
Post Box 4109
New Delhi 110 017 India

Printed in the United States of America

Library of Congress Cataloging-in-Publication Data

Schneider, Joe.
The principal's guide to managing communication/E. Joseph Schneider,
Lara L. Hollenczer.
    p. cm.—(Leadership for learning)
Includes bibliographical references and index.
ISBN 1–4129–1462–0 (cloth)—ISBN 1–4129–1463–9 (pbk.)
    1. Communication in education. 2. Educational leadership.
I. Hollenczer, Lara L. II. Title. III. Series.
LB1033.5.S36 2006
371.102′2—dc22   2005019

This book is printed on acid-free paper.

06   07   08   09   10   9   8   7   6   5   4   3   2   1

Acquisitions Editor:	Rachel Livsey
Editorial Assistant:	Phyllis Cappello
Production Editor:	Beth A. Bernstein
Copy Editor:	Dan Hays
Typesetter:	C&M Digitals (P) Ltd.
Proofreader:	Colleen Brennan
Indexer:	Sylvia Coates
Cover Designer:	Rose Storey

Dedicated to

Robert R. Rath

He taught us a thing or two about communication management.

Contents

List of Tables and Figures

Series Foreword

Never before has it been as important for school leaders to communicate effectively with their stakeholders, including students, teachers, families, community leaders, and the public. This is not a matter of selling the message or gaining political support or heading off opposition. Indeed, if these goals shape the communication strategy of a school, it is almost certainly going to be ineffective—if not counterproductive.

Drawing on research on private, as well as public, organizations, and drawing on decades of experience, E. Joseph Schneider and Lara L. Hollenczer provide school leaders with ways of thinking and acting strategically to build partnerships that will enhance the contributions schools can make to student learning.

The strategic approach to "communication management" that Schneider and Hollenczer describe recognizes that schools cannot do their job without both the support of families and others that influence student learning and the ideas and information they can provide. The "management" of communications is essential because there is a great deal of information to which the schools' stakeholders have access, and they have limited time and interest in sorting out what they really need to know and what they have learned that is not true or otherwise misleading.

Managing communication does not mean manipulating information, however. It means carefully planning to inform and to learn from stakeholders in the school's effectiveness to ensure that all children learn at high levels. Chester Barnard, said by some to be one of the pioneers of thinking about organizations, argued in 1938 that businesses need to think about those on whom the success of the company depends (e.g., clients) as members of the organization. In successful organizations, members need to be well informed, have the capacity to understand one another, trust that what they are learning is truthful, and know that their ideas are sought and respected. That understanding guides the strategic approach to communication advocated in this unique book.

—*Willis D. Hawley*

Series
Introduction

The American Association of School Administrators (AASA) is the largest association in the world representing school system leaders and, in particular, school district superintendents. These educational leaders know that the quality of America's schools depends heavily on the ability of school principals. AASA recognizes a pressing need exists to improve the skills and knowledge of current and prospective school leaders. To help address this need, AASA has put in place the Leadership for Learning initiative. This series of books plays a central role in this initiative.

The Leadership for Learning books address a broad range of knowledge and skills school superintendents, exceptional principals, and researchers believe are essential to ensure effective leadership at the school level. The content of this series of books reflects the "leaders' standards" developed for state licensure by the Interstate School Leaders Licensure Consortium (ISLLC), which is composed of representatives from several professional organizations representing educators, policymakers, and scholars. These standards have been adopted by more than two thirds of the states as the criteria by which the qualifications of school principals should be judged. Although the books in the series can be thought of as parts of a coherent curriculum, individual books stand on their own as syntheses of relevant research and expert consensus about best practice. The series as a whole reflects these commitments:

- All students should have the opportunity to maximize their potential for intellectual and social development.
- Enhancing the quality of teaching is the most important way to influence students' opportunities to learn.

- The actions of administrators, teachers, and school staff should be based on collaborative problem solving focused on the systematic analysis of student performance and evidence of effective practice.
- School leaders need to foster the active engagement of parents and community organizations in the direct facilitation of student learning.

Never before has it been as important for school leaders to communicate effectively with their stakeholders—including students, teachers, families, community leaders and the public. This is not a matter of selling the message or gaining political support or heading off opposition. Indeed, if these goals shape the communication strategy of a school, it is almost certainly going to be ineffective—if not counter-productive.

Drawing on research on private, as well as public, organizations, and drawing on decades of experience, E. Joseph Schneider provides school leaders with ways of thinking and acting strategically to build partnerships that will enhance the contributions schools can make to student learning.

The strategic approach to "communication management" that Schneider describes recognizes that schools cannot do their job without both the support of families and others that influence student learning and the ideas and information they can provide. The "management" of communications is essential because there is a great deal of information to which the schools' stakeholders have access and they have limited time and interest in sorting out what they really need to know and what they have learned that is not true or otherwise misleading.

But managing communication does not mean manipulating information. It means carefully planning to inform and to learn from stakeholders in the school's effectiveness in order to ensure that all children learn at high levels. Chester Barnard, said by some to be one of the pioneers of thinking about organizations, argued in 1938 that businesses need to think about those on whom the success of the company depends (e.g., clients) as members of the organization. In successful organizations, members need to be well informed, have the capacity to understand one another, trust that what they are learning is truthful, and know what their ideas are sought and respected. That understanding guides the strategic approach to communication advocated in this unique book.

—*Willis D. Hawley*
Series Editor

Preface

Everyone thinking about becoming a school leader knows they had better sharpen their communication skills. It goes with the job. Principals spend a good portion of their day communicating with stakeholders, including staff, teachers, students, parents, central office administrators, and the superintendent. Schools today are expected to be transparent places. Data about state-administered test scores are public information, and school-by-school comparisons are published in the local newspaper. Principals are asked to explain the differences in scores. Students walk around with cell phones supposedly turned off, but let anything out of the ordinary occur on campus and the information is shared citywide in a heartbeat. And harried calls come immediately back to the principal for comment and clarification.

A transparent school requires principals to be much more open in their leadership style too. Consequently, principals today learn to delegate, to plan with committees of teachers and parents and even students. Trust and respect are built among the Partners, and a bond forms so that all parties are working together to help ensure the best education possible for the children in the school. The principal provides the leadership to keep the partnership moving ahead. But the partnership is dependent on the buy-in of its members. And they stay committed to the partnership because they believe the principal is as committed to the partnership as they are. In other words, they respect and trust him: He is their principal.

Therein lies another communication challenge for the principal. While fortifying his ties to his school partners, he may well be weakening his links to his employer, the superintendent, and central office staff that surround him.

In this era in which principals are being encouraged to develop a new leadership style that emphasizes instructional leadership and stronger ties to teachers, family, and community, there is a danger that principals might weaken their ties to their employer.

Simply put, principals are being trained to see themselves as leaders of their schools. They are being told they are responsible for the school's success, and they certainly are being held accountable for the children's achievement. As such, take-charge principals are enlisting faculty and family as well as community and students in an all-out effort to collectively address the school's academic needs. They are doing what it takes to get the job done.

But the fact is that principals are midlevel managers in larger bureaucracy. They report to someone in the central office. It may be directly to the superintendent in a small district, or it may be an assistant superintendent in a larger district. But in most districts, several people above the school level believe they have the authority to tell principals what to do. They in turn are told what to do by the school board, and it in turn is ordered around by the State Board of Education and the U.S. Department of Education. The question openly asked today is "Who really does run America's public schools?" Nobody really thinks it is the school principal.

That is why this book was written. Principals are required to please many people. It can be done, but it requires extraordinary communication management skills.

It is one thing to understand communication. It is another thing to understand it in context with management. Principals need to know how to manage communications among and between their various stakeholders if they are going to be effective at leading their schools.

From this book, principals will learn enough theory so they understand the how as well as the why when they use a strategy that enables them to deliver a top-down, district-ordered message to their schools' teachers, parents, and community and still maintain a collegial, working relationship with them. Or how best to word an argument to take to the central office for why a district policy should not go forward because it would interfere with plans the school has for its own self-improvement.

Interestingly, the literature for blending communication and management together derives from a field that at first blush probably would make most seasoned educational administrators skittish. It is public relations. School administrators tend to become nervous when authors start proposing public relations as a solution to their management challenges. The very term conjures up images of press agents and speech writers and, worst of all, educational consultants. School leaders associate the term with propaganda and manipulation, and they just do not want anything to do with it. Well, that is not how the term is used here. Public relations is defined in this book as simply the "management of communications between an organization and its publics."

Throughout the book, public relations is talked about as the management of the communication that occurs between the school and its stakeholders. That is the public relations function. It is a management function, and it is the principals' responsibility. Principals cannot be effective leaders unless they also effectively manage the communication between their schools and their schools' stakeholders.

Key to every principal's success will be mastering the management of the communication between her school and her two key audiences: the enablers and the Partners. Simply stated, the Enablers are those people with the authority to tell the principal what to do. In other words, Enablers are those with the power to have the principal removed from her position. The Partners are those people with the ability to help or hinder the principal in her efforts to accomplish her school's goals.

Consequently, the primary thing school leaders will gain from reading this book is the ability to manage the communication between themselves and their key stakeholders so they can achieve their major objectives for their schools.

Organization of the Book

The book is organized into two parts. Part I provides the reader with an understanding of the theory that undergirds communication management. From these four chapters, readers will gain keen insights into stakeholders and publics and how a principal should attempt to manage communication with them. The theory comes from the public relations literature; much flows from the work of Professor James E. Grunig of the University of Maryland and his colleagues.

In Chapter 1, the reader is shown how principals go about identifying their schools' stakeholders. Furthermore, they are told that the more critical issue is to figure out who among their stakeholders will be "publics." These are groups of people that form in response to issues or problems. Stakeholders groups are "latent," which are basically paying no attention to the problem or issue; "aware," which are aware but not doing anything about the problem or issue yet; and "active," which are aware of the problem or issue and are actively engaged to do something about it. Each public has a different communication behavior, which means that principals have to be sensitive to the various ways they process or seek out information if communicating with them is going to be successful.

Chapter 2 introduces the reader to Grunig's "situational theory to identify publics." It provides the reader with an understanding of why it is so challenging for principals to engage their various stakeholder publics in meaningful communication. More critically, the chapter spells out some clear implications of the theory for how school leaders should operate a communication management program.

Chapter 3 brings the reader into the heart of the book. This chapter introduces principals to the four most generally used communication management models and suggests most districts and schools cling to the "public information model" in which communication is basically one-way, from the school to the public, with little regard for how it is received. In a transparent school environment in which leadership is diffused and information widely available, a better communication model is one in which the school and its stakeholders are both engaged in a give-and-take exchange. The book explains why this model is preferred for principals today and how they should use it. The book also explains why, given the fact that school principals are still district-level employees, the model does not always work. Consequently, the book introduces principals to another model: the "mixed-motive" approach. The chapter goes on to explain when principals should use this alternative and cites the risks associated with its use. Although risky, the mixed-motive approach is probably going to be used frequently by the top principals as they attempt to balance the needs of both their Enablers and their Partners.

Chapter 4, the closing chapter of Part I, is an important one. It outlines the rationale behind the school-family-community partnerships and introduces the reader to the six major types of involvement that generally make up such an arrangement. This chapter borrows extensively from the work of Joyce Epstein and colleagues at the Center for Social Organization of Schools at The Johns Hopkins University. It is critical that school leaders learn what it takes to start such partnerships at whatever level of school—elementary, middle, or secondary—they intend to provide leadership.

Chapter 5 begins Part II of the book by offering the school leader a chance to read three case studies featuring an elementary, a middle, and a secondary school principal who used communication management strategies on the job. By reading these case studies, the school leader will have an opportunity to review the theories learned in the previous chapters and get a glimpse of their practical application. The chapter also makes the point that the best lessons are frequently taught by peers.

Chapter 6 reminds the new school leader that not all communication originates from the principal's office. The principal's office is often the recipient of the communication. Knowing how to listen, negotiate, and compromise are all communication skills an effective principal masters. This chapter highlights some of the more common issues that confront principals and suggests how they might deal with them.

Chapter 7 suggests that principals with good communication management skills can play significant roles in their respective districts. On the one hand, they can be called on by their districts to be "boundary spanners" because they are close to the stakeholders. Consequently, they are able to read the public mood and give district-level administrators some early indication about how certain stakeholders would receive news of a new district-imposed policy. On the other hand, the district may choose to use such principals as part of the administrative decision-making team, calling on their insights and links to the stakeholders to enlighten the process at the central office. This chapter concludes with a suggestion to new school leaders that they master the ability to read and understand data.

Chapter 8 is a nuts-and-bolts chapter outlining the various tools that principals can use when managing communication. The chapter is particularly concerned with Web sites, e-mail, and other electronic devices now popular with stakeholders.

Chapter 9 moves the reader into some of the more practical applications of communication management. Here, the reader receives a basic primer in "communication" that every new principal should master before accepting the position. The chapter covers the basics; for example, it examines what communication tools are appropriate to use, in which situations, for which audiences.

Chapter 10 closes the book with a concluding statement.

Acknowledgments

My coauthor, Lara Hollenczer, and I owe a dept of gratitude to the many school leaders who helped us bring this book to life. Among these were friends of mine from the University of Oregon, Max G. Abbott and Lloyd DuVall; and Richard Rossmiller, a long-time chair of the Department of Educational Administration at the University of Wisconsin, Madison. Although I never took a course from any of them, I worked on the boundaries of their profession for more than 30 years and learned much from them. Others who contributed to my understanding of school leaders were Robert R. Rath, the long-time executive director of the Northwest Regional Educational Laboratory in Portland, Oregon, and James Becker and Robert Scanlon, both previous executive directors of Research for Better Schools in Philadelphia. All six of these former principals and R&D leaders were chairmen of the board of directors of the Council for Educational Development and Research in Washington, D.C., while I was its executive director.

While working at the American Association of School Administrators (AASA), I had the opportunity to get to know many outstanding superintendents, all of whom had previously been school principals. I called on them liberally when writing this book. I owe a debt of gratitude to Stephen W. Daeschner, superintendent of Jefferson County, Kentucky, public schools. A couple of times when I got stumped and had a question, he allowed me to interrupt his incredibly busy day and provided me with an explanation. Another former principal who was generous in his guidance and insights was Joseph J. Cirasuolo, retired superintendent from Connecticut and past president of AASA. Joe read an early draft of one of the chapters and provided helpful feedback. I also did not hesitate to pick the brain of my good friend Thomas F. Koerner, retired executive director of the National Association of Secondary School Principals. A popular secondary principal, Richard Warner, from my hometown of Fargo, North Dakota, also met with me to discuss the principalship. A case study featuring Dick is one of the book's highlights.

Lara and I owe a particular dept of graduate to Anne Turnburgh Lockwood, a fellow author for Corwin who guided us through the editing mysteries of the publishing world. Anne, an accomplished writer in her own right, read an early version of the manuscript and offered numerous suggestions for improvement. Willis Hawley, the coeditor of the Leadership for Learning Series of which this book is a part, also read and commented on several early drafts; his feedback also was invaluable. A final thanks to Rachel Livsey, acquisitions editor at Corwin Press, who guided this project from start to finish.

Finally, we could not have written this book without the public relations research done by James E. Grunig, professor of communications at the University of Maryland, College Park. Although he was helpful in providing us with books and finding us refuge copies of hard-to-trace original sources quoted in his seminal text, we did not ask him to review our book; consequently, he has no burden of responsibility for any mistakes we might have made in the application of his theory to the field of educational leadership.

Corwin Press gratefully acknowledges the contribution of the following reviewers:

Richard B. Warner
Assistant Professor
School of Education
North Dakota State University
Fargo, ND

Susan N. Imamura
Principal
Manoa Elementary School
Honolulu, HI

Kathryn Anderson Alvestad
Adjunct Associate Professor
University of Maryland
College Park, MD

Robert Ramsey
Associate Superintendent (retired)
Education Consultant
Minneapolis, MN

Mike Ford
Superintendent of Schools
Phelps-Clifton Springs Central School District
Clifton Springs, NY

Susan Stone Kessler
Assistant Principal
Hillsboro High School
Metropolitan Nashville Public Schools
Nashville, TN

About the Authors

 **E. Joseph Schneider** has been in education for more than 30 years as an association executive, research manager, and communication director. He is Managing Partner of Leadership Development Resources, an educational consulting company based in Arlington, Virginia. Concurrently, he also serves as executive secretary of the National Policy Board for Educational Administration, a coalition of ten national education associations concerned about educational leadership. Previously, he was the deputy executive director of the American Association of School Administrators (AASA), the national membership association of school superintendents. Prior to that, he was the deputy executive director of the Southwest Regional Educational Laboratory, Los Alamitos, California. He also has 15 years of experience as the CEO of a Washington, D.C., education association whose members are university-based research centers and nonprofit educational research and development agencies. His master's degree in journalism is from the University of Oregon. He is a member of the National School Public Relations Association. He is coauthor of *The Unauthorized Communication Handbook* (1991) and *Exploding the Myths: Another Round in the Education Debate* (with Paul D. Houston) (1993). He has also written more than 100 education-related journal, magazine, and newsletter articles. His latest book, coauthored with Ronald G. Corwin, is *The School Choice Hoax: Fixing America's Schools* (2005).

 **Lara L. Hollenczer**, the mother of two public school youngsters, is heavily involved in local educational issues as a parent, community activist, and local business owner. Professionally, she made her mark by helping law firms harness the capacity of the Internet for "branding" their firms, conducting market research, and developing new clients. After stints at several large Washington, D.C., law firms, she joined a fast-growing Annapolis, Maryland, advertising and public relations agency where her clients included local and state teacher associations. After several years at the agency, she expanded her business to assist clients with research, market development, and media planning. She is accredited in public relations with the Public Relations Society of America and is a Professional Certified Marketer with the American Marketing Association. Her master's degree is in communication management from Syracuse University.

PART I

Understanding Stakeholders and Publics

Principals have always had communication responsibilities. Throughout most of the 20th century, superintendents hired principals and told them their job was to make sure the stakeholders had confidence in their schools. Key to this, of course, was implanting in people's minds favorable images of the schools, their students, faculty, the academic programs, and, of course, the principals. Just about anything positive associated with the schools was fodder for principals to consider when communicating with their schools' stakeholders.

The idea, principals knew, was to tell good things about their schools and play down or ignore the bad. Principals who earned reputations as strong advocates for their schools were said to have "good communication skills." To hone them, nearly every communication book of the era targeted to school principals focused on ways they could improve these skills. For example, these books taught principals how to use the local media to get the school more coverage, how to run meetings effectively, how to select the right words for letters, how to talk to parents, and how to address parent groups.

The assumption underlying this decades-old communication strategy, borrowed from business and industry, was that good will builds up over time. Accumulate enough, and a manager should be able to weather an occasional crisis.

As comforting as that assumption has always been to management, it always proves to be only partially true. Educators learned this lesson the hard way in 1983 when the U.S. Department of Education released its *Nation at Risk* report. It boldly declared that public schools throughout the United States had failed to accomplish their purpose, and a large segment of the public believed every word of it. So much for years of school administrators gently reassuring their stakeholders about the worth of public schools.

One thing became painfully evident to a distraught educational community after the report's widespread dissemination: Simply telling stakeholders about all the good things going on at their schools was not going to be a sufficient communication strategy anymore.

Grudgingly, many educators began to concede that improvements were probably overdue, even if the public schools were not nearly as bad as the critics were suggesting. For one thing, there was a clear expectation that educators were going to be held accountable for educating all the children that came to school, and accountability for student achievement was now assigned to the school principal.

Principals' Roles Have Changed

Superintendents used to hire principals to "run schools." Now superintendents talk about recruiting "instructional leaders." The days when superintendents were content to have principals operating as midlevel managers, implementing districtwide policy, maintaining buildings, and passing along top-down communication to the community are over. Nobody talks about the principals "managing" schools anymore. Today, it is all about "leadership." That is, leaders are expected to have a vision for their schools and to be the sources of ideas for achieving these visions. But principals are no longer in a position in which they can assume their ideas will prevail through fiat and authority. They must now learn to encourage the participation of their school's stakeholders in partnerships to fulfill these visions. Some of these Partners, however, will be tentative; others will be difficult to engage; and some will be self-serving and see the principal's vision as counter to their best interests. Consequently, the principals' changing role requires that they learn different management skills than their predecessors may have needed. One of the new skill sets that leaders must have is a mastery of communication management.

That mastery begins with insight into "stakeholder" groups and the "publics" within these groups.

1

Who Are the Stakeholders and Publics in Your School?

Years ago, when principals only had to concern themselves with passing down messages from their schools to their stakeholders, the communication management function depended to a large extent on the maintenance of good mailing lists. Savvy principals would make sure that their schools had up-to-date lists of all their key stakeholders, complete with phone numbers and mailing addresses.

Nobody could ever be sure that the materials sent out were read. No matter. The principals always had their lists. If necessary, they could prove the mailings had gone out. That is what was important. Many of the mailings were dictated by district or state mandates. Many were designed to solicit a response. "You can bring a horse to water, but you can't make it drink," used to be a common explanation for a light response to a district mailing.

What the principal missed, of course, was the fact that most of the stakeholders who received these mailings simply did not recognize the issue being discussed as significant enough to warrant their attention. Or if they did, the information provided did not explain how they could get involved to address the issue. Or, as likely, most of the people who received the mailing probably did not feel much involved with the school anyway, so they simply read the message, pitched the brochure, and proceeded to forget what they read in short order.

Connecting with a school's stakeholders is not any easier today than it ever was. In fact, it probably is tougher than ever—but it can be done, especially if principals employ the strategies covered in this book.

It Takes Two to Communicate

School principals are well aware of the fact that they need to communicate with various "stakeholders." They know they constitute a vast network of individuals who have an investment of one kind or another in the schools. For many of these stakeholders, their links to the schools are formal. For example, many are school employees. Teachers, support staff, and fellow administrators are all stakeholders. But so are students. Parents are stakeholders, too. The superintendent and members of the school board are stakeholders as well.

Stakeholders also can have less formal links to the school. So add members of the community to the list of stakeholders, as well as representatives of the local media, neighbors who live down the street from the school, and the individuals who sell meat and potatoes to the cafeteria. The number of stakeholders can be staggering. In a small community, with a single K–12 school, everyone is a stakeholder. In a large suburb, the stakeholders for a single school may be greater in number, even if they are more geographically bound.

Although communicating with stakeholders is an important part of a principal's job, many do it rather ineffectively. That is because communication takes both parties to make the process work. For many of the school's stakeholders, communicating with the principal requires more interest than they have, more involvement than they are willing to make, and more time to retain information than they have.

Other stakeholders may feel only marginally connected to the school and consequently tend to ignore or forget nearly everything they hear about it. Still others brush off the principal's efforts to communicate because they do not believe their involvement with the school would make any difference anyway.

Public schools are among the many public institutions that the public no longer feels they have to take any responsibility for. Decades of school administrators communicated to them the message that the public schools were in capable hands and did not need the public's involvement, just their support. Public Agenda discovered that two thirds of their respondents said they were comfortable leaving school policies for educators to decide (Farkas, Foley, & Duffett, 2001, p. 15). It is quite possible that the public no longer believes that the public schools are their schools. As federal and state governments have become increasingly involved in setting policies for neighborhood schools, local taxpayers could easily feel the need for their involvement has all but disappeared.

In this era of technology, some will argue for e-mail messages and Web site postings to get community engagement. Others will say nothing beats personal phone calls or face-to-face meetings. Still other principals will argue that they have tried them all, and one approach will work one time and fail miserably another time. Principals are frequently urged to get good news stories published in the local paper. That seems to make sense. When asked whether a good news story about the school offset a bad news story about the school, however, they are not sure. What is a principal to do?

Of course, if all principals had to worry about was how to convince stakeholders to process their communication, this book would be much thinner than it is. Many stakeholders are concerned about what is going on at the local school and do not rely on the principal as their primary source of information about it. These stakeholders will get their news elsewhere, sit around with their peers digesting its meaning, and then will want a showdown session with the principal to get to the bottom of things. Sometimes, the problem they want to talk about has not even surfaced on the principal's radar screen yet.

Stakeholders Are People With Links to the Schools

Stakeholders are people linked to an organization. They are linked because they and the organization have consequences on each other—they cause problems for each other. People linked to an organization have a stake in it, which Carroll (1989) defined as "an interest or a share in an undertaking" (p. 56). A stakeholder, therefore, is "any individual or group who can affect or is affected by the actions, decisions, policies, practices, or goals of the organization" (Freeman, 1984, p. 25).

For example, the school board, superintendent, central office, and other officials who have power over the school constitute a group of stakeholders. All the school's employees can constitute a stakeholder group. Still another group may be dominated by parents but includes

Figure 1.1   The principal manages the communication between the principal's office and the school's various stakeholders.

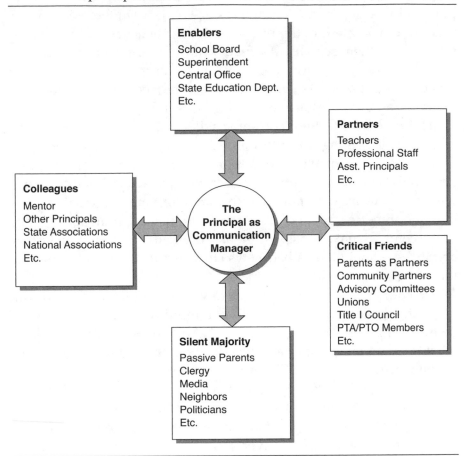

PTA/PTO members, school volunteers, and reading tutors. Together, these are principals' major stakeholders with whom they will have their most frequent communication interactions. The largest category, though, includes politicians, members of the media, residents of the neighborhood, and others who only tangentially touch the school. A final category consists of the principal's mentors, friends, fellow principals, and colleagues from state and national associations.

The stakeholder groups are fluid in that they contract and expand all the time. Nevertheless, each of these major groups has a name, as Figure 1.1 illustrates.

The first step in any effort to be strategic about communication management is to establish a "stakeholders' map" for a school. The map is a starting point for organizing the school's individual stakeholders into various categories so that principals can rank or assign them to groups to indicate their impact on their schools or the extent to which their schools believe they should pay attention to them. In the case of public schools, this grouping generally produces five broad categories of stakeholders.

Enablers

Enablers are those individuals who can fire principals or make their lives so miserable that they are likely to quit if pressured. The list of Enablers varies from city to city as the nation struggles to figure out who is in charge of the public schools. In some large cities, the mayors and state governors play a central role along with state commissioners of education and state boards of education in the operation of the public schools. For example, in Rhode Island in February 2005, the state commissioner of education personally ordered a Providence high school to reevaluate all its teachers and administrators to decide who should be transferred from the building (Archer, 2005). Although such hands-on intervention from the state level is unusual, principals should not be surprised to find they confront an ever-expanding list of Enablers.

In a small town, school principals' Enablers may be prominent ministers, the owner of a company that employs many of the town's people, or perhaps the president of the local college or even newspaper editors. Even in cities the size of New York or Los Angeles, however, it is not uncommon for the mayors to get involved in school-related issues and dictate to the board of education how it should conduct its business right down to dictating how individual schools should operate. Enablers, in other words, are the powerbrokers who issue orders to principals or, in many cases, they are the people who influence the officials who officially issue the orders to the building-level administrators.

Principals do not need to read a handbook to know it is important to pay attention to the communication that comes out of the central office. But it is also important for principals to understand that they need to pay some attention to the communication flow back to the central office.

Principals will want to pay attention to what comes down from the central office. As an employee of the district, the principal works for an Enabler, the superintendent of schools, or one of the superintendent's top administrators. So there is a chain of command in addition to a communication loop operating between the school and the central office that is key. Many of the issues and problems that impact the school originate as policy directives and mandates that originate in the central office or come through the central office from state or federal governments. Principals need to understand these policies and mandates. They need to understand the reasoning behind them, the laws that buttress them, and the recourse, if any, for those who may wish to reject or oppose them. Only then can the principal be in a position to communicate effectively about them with the school's other stakeholders.

Partners

Having said Enablers were the key stakeholder group, an equally strong argument could be made on behalf of Partners. These are the teachers, professional staff, assistant principals, and other personnel from within the school. But Partners also include family members, including parents, grandparents, and others involved in the lives of the children who attend the school. This group includes those community members involved in civic, counseling, cultural, health, recreation, and other agencies and organizations and businesses that strengthen the school's programs or family practices and foster student learning and development.

The term *Partners* is used intentionally to convey a particular kind of relationship among school, families, and communities. Epstein et al. (2002) noted,

> Partners can improve school programs and school climate, provide family services and support, increase parent skills and leadership, connect families with others in the school and in the community, and help teachers with their work. However, the main reason to create a partnership is to help all youngsters succeed in school and in later life. (p. 7)

A quality school is characterized by a principal and a staff that distribute leadership, trust one another, and openly communicate about issues and problems. Individuals who have this relationship with principals constitute their core "Partners."

Because they are in the building together, engaged in the same rituals, practices, and routines, Partners and principals should not have many secrets from one another. But that does not mean formal communication is unnecessary. Most schools have a vicious grapevine that spreads "news" rapidly through the faculty and custodial staff, so formal communication may not seem necessary to get information around the building. Principals who rely on the grapevine as their communication channel are not being particularly strategic, however, especially when dealing with Partners who tend to cluster on both ends of the agree-disagree continuum. Simply put, strategic principals want to put as much of their communication in writing as possible to formalize it, particularly concerning sensitive or emotional issues. This ensures accuracy. That way, principals and their supporters can be assured they are working off the same page when the message gets repeated to others. Those who may disagree with the principals will at least have to argue facts, not hearsay.

The rumor mill or grapevine will always spew information, and the Partners will avail themselves to it if the principal communicates with them or not. But unless the principal officially explains what or why something is affecting the school's stakeholders, and particularly its Partners, then someone else is likely to cook up an "official" explanation. It is seldom in the principal's best interest to let someone else do the explaining for him or her.

Box 1.1   Cultivating Your Grapevine

Most researchers agree that the rumor mill is as old as time—and that it was dubbed the grapevine in popular speech after wires were strung cross-country in the mid-1800s to power the new-fangled telegraph. Telegrams have long since been abandoned as a primary method of rapid communication, but the organizational grapevine is as alive as ever.

It is a good bet that you will never eliminate the active grapevine in your schools and communities. Whether your grapevine yields sour grapes or fine wine depends on how well you care for and feed it. Consider what the research tells us.

Many employees have been conditioned to believe that if something is really important, they will probably hear about it on the grapevine first. The grapevine is a real and important communication tool for most organizations. Also, grapevines are viable at all levels of an organization—from top to bottom. But they may not all intersect with one another.

Result: Know how information informally flows throughout your organization and your communities, and have ways to get information to these networks when needed.

Rumors

Some people are more prone than others to spread rumors on a grapevine. But how listeners respond to the information depends a great deal on the organization's history. If the organization, particularly frontline communicators (e.g., principals or administrative assistants), is known for being accessible and forthright, people will be more likely to check out information with such authoritative sources before believing it and spreading the gossip.

Result: Train your staff in the importance of listening to the grapevine and addressing key issues as they emerge. They need to appreciate that even their inaction in addressing a rumor may be interpreted by some as evidence that it "must be true."

Credibility

The credibility of the source of any message has a great deal to do with whether or not it is accepted and believed—in both formal communication tactics and informal ones, such as a grapevine. In some cases, superintendents and board members may not enjoy as much credibility with some audiences as building principals or community members. In such cases, certain messages may be better delivered by these people alone or in joint presentations with a superintendent or board members.

Lesson: It is important to strategize who will deliver certain messages, not just what the message will be (National School Public Relations Association, 2004).

Going silent with Partners is always a mistake on the part of a principal. If the principal has not been communicating with them, the Partners will go to external sources to get information and to express their views. Sources of information, and outlets for their views, include their unions, the central office, the media, interest groups, and parents. In other words, before they know it, the principals are out of the communication loop with the very folks everyone would expect to be their closest allies. When that happens, the principal's effectiveness as a leader will be sorely questioned.

The lesson here is to never take Partners for granted. Although principals pass them in the hall daily, meet with them regularly, and read the same memos from the central office that they do, principals should never assume they "got the message." Likewise, principals should never assume Partners can be kept out of the information loop. They expect to hear from the school's leader on matters affecting the school and to hear about it early, often, and thoroughly. Also, Partners want the school's leader to listen to them in turn. Principals spend a large percentage of their communication management time engaged in dialogue with their Partners. The time is always well spent. Partners are frequently conduits for other stakeholders; consequently, the better informed the Partners, the better the information flow to the broader audience.

Silent Majority

The overworked label, "silent majority," is applied to the largest category of stakeholders for the simple reason that it sticks so well. This group, the majority of the school's stakeholders, is for the most part silent when it comes to communication. That is, this group is not likely to ever go seeking information or to process information it receives about the school. If the principal attempts to communicate with members of the group, the effort will for the most part be a waste of time and resources.

Does this mean the principal can simply ignore this group of stakeholders? No, it is not that simple. Some of the majority should not be silent. They just do not realize it. It is the principal's job to convince them to start communicating about what is going on at the school.

At the top of that list is passive parents and other family members of the students in the schools. Unfortunately, not every parent is a member of the school's partnership, although they should be. Principals would like them to be. If principals could wish it to happen, they would be. Part of every principal's communication plan should be a strategy to woo the parents from the Silent Majority camp into a partnership group. How that might be done is discussed in a later chapter. Simply stated, the more involved a person becomes in school activities, the less likely that person is to feel constrained about being able to make a difference and the more likely that person is to seek information about the school.

Everyone who has even a tangential link to the school is a member of the silent majority. Imagine a district with a retired couple living across the street from a school. The couple has never visited the school, never enrolled a child in it, or never given it much thought. The couple is one of the school's Silent Majority. Obviously, that school's principal should not spend much of her limited printing and mailing budget stuffing brochures and pamphlets into the couple's mailbox. It would serve no purpose. A principal should never completely turn a deaf ear to the Silent Majority, however, because its members could quickly become a hostile "vocal minority."

Returning to our district in which the school board has decided to increase the enrollment in one of its schools next year and to place portable classrooms in its playground, a prediction is possible. The retired couple living close to the school might be expected to be angry when they hear the news. They are likely to claim that their property value will fall; that more school buses on the street will interfere with and create a safety hazard for their own driving; that the extra students attending the new modules will increase the noise level in the neighborhood, which will in turn disturb their pets; and, of course, that they were not consulted. This "one-issue" public will exist until the problem goes away or their concern is addressed. Then they will return to the ranks of the Silent Majority. In the meantime, however, they will be actively engaged in a public hostile to the school's interests and doing their best to get the principal to focus his time and energy on their single issue.

Others within the Silent Majority are individuals the school would like to have as allies if not partners, such as the media. Every principal wants the education reporters as friends of their school. If the local media can afford to put reporters full-time on the education beat, however, it is probably because the community has many schools. That means there are many principals seeking to be the reporters' friends. It can be done, though, and some tips will be offered later.

The point is that the Silent Majority contains a large number of people. Some logically belong in the principal's partnership category. Part of what a principal's communication strategy is all about is identifying people by name within the Silent Majority and then working the communication model to move them gently over to the Partnership category. Keep in mind that the move requires them to boost their awareness of the school first. Then, ever so gently, the principal should help increase their level of involvement with the school. Once that occurs—presto—the principal has more names to add to the partnership stakeholder lists.

Colleagues

All school principals have Friends. They are members of their Stakeholder group. They tend to give honest feedback, have no axe to grind, and have the principals' best interests at heart. For that reason alone, they are a pleasure to communicate with. In addition, they generally know what the principals are going through, so they have empathy, can offer advice, and provide solace. Principals need to surround themselves with trusted Friends. A mentor is important. Fortunately, most principals come into the job with one. In many cases, it is a veteran school administrator or a university professor.

If principals do not have one, they should get one. It is probably easier than they think. If they are new principals, then they should ask their supervisors or superintendents to be paired with principals in their districts. The word "mentor" never has to be used. The new principals should simply say they would like their supervisors' opinion of who they could best learn the ropes from by observing their schools, attending their staff meetings on occasion, or picking up the phone and asking a question from time to time.

If the district is small and a principal needs a mentor, she might ask the executive director of her state's principal association to match her up with one or two top principals in her county or area of the state. New principals do not need to be shy; the top principals were all first-year principals at one time too.

Other principals are also a key part of a principal's network. In communities served by more than one school, members of one school's stakeholder group overlap with those of another's stakeholder group. They may all share the same media, for example, and obviously the same school board, superintendent, and central office. So it behooves principals to stay in the loop with their administrator colleagues. Also, secondary school principals always want to know what the principals of the middle or junior high schools, or even the principals of elementary schools, that make up their feeder schools are picking up from their stakeholder groups that may impact their schools. The reverse is also true. A cunning principal communicates carefully but continually with his circle of compadres.

Identifying "Publics" Among Stakeholders

Principals communicate regularly with their stakeholders about all kinds of school-related information, and it does not strike anyone as anything out of the ordinary. School lunch menus are posted on the Web site, upcoming school events are announced, teacher appointments are made, and school closing dates are scheduled. Most of this communication comes from the principal's office to the stakeholders in the customary top-down manner for which bureaucratic organizations are famous and yet few, if any, of the stakeholders would want it any other way. The principal is expected to generate such communication.

The principal does not need to be too concerned with the management of the day-to-day routine flow of communication from the principal's office to the stakeholders. That is something every principal and a good administrative assistant can work out between themselves within the first year on the job.

What principals need to be concerned about is the management of information when there is a problem or issue. Because when there is a problem or issue—the words can probably be used interchangeably, but in educational circles they sometimes take on different meanings—the communication challenge increases.

The reason the challenge increases is because the presence of a problem or issue creates a public. In 1938, John Dewey defined a public as "a group of people who (a) face a similar problem; (b) recognize that the problem exists; and (3) organize to do something about the problem" (as quoted in Grunig & Hunt, 1984, p. 145; Figure 1.2). Since Dewey defined a public, Grunig and Hunt have posited that there are really four kinds of publics:

1. Aware publics: Stakeholders who face a similar situation or problem and recognize it as such.

2. Active publics: Stakeholders who face an issue or problem, recognize it, and organize to take some action.

3. Latent publics: Stakeholders who are confronted with an issue or problem but do not recognize its existence.

4. Nonpublics: Stakeholders who are faced with an issue or problem but remain unaware of or unconcerned about its existence.

To illustrate how publics within stakeholder groups form around an issue, think of a state department of education that will soon release test scores for a school. The scores will show that the students, on average, did well. This will come as no surprise to its stakeholders because the school has a reputation for excellence. The

Figure 1.2   The school's stakeholders make up three different kinds of publics with three different kinds of communication behavior.

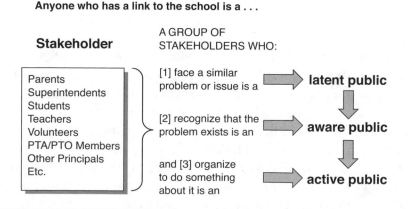

Anyone who has a link to the school is a . . .

Stakeholder

A GROUP OF STAKEHOLDERS WHO:

Parents
Superintendents
Students
Teachers
Volunteers
PTA/PTO Members
Other Principals
Etc.

[1] face a similar problem or issue is a ➡ **latent public**

[2] recognize that the problem exists is an ➡ **aware public**

and [3] organize to do something about it is an ➡ **active public** data also show, however, that the special education students scored below the state average for special education students on the exams and did not meet minimum state requirements. Consequently, the school is going to be put on "probation." It is definitely a black eye for the principal and his faculty, and when the news is released it will cause uproar among several of his Partners and generate media inquiries about the quality of his instructional program. When the press covers the story, the neighbors living near the school certainly will hear about it.

For this illustration, four publics composed of stakeholders are involved: the school faculty, the parents of the special education students in the school, the local media, and the neighbors living near the school. These publics include those that can be described as aware, latent, and nonpublic. Potentially, each may become an active public, and some parents of special education student are invariably active.

The first two audiences, school faculty and special education parents, are aware publics because they knew the students had been tested. They realize that the state department will release the findings, and they are awaiting information about the results and poised to be become active publics. As such, they are receptive to an official explanation about the test scores. Had the principal not provided an explanation that made sense to these two publics, however, as active publics, they would have sought out other information sources, conversed among themselves, and undoubtedly found someone or something to blame for the poor scores.

Before the release of information, the media were a latent public—that is, a "dormant" or a "docile" public. They recognized that the state had tested the students but were relying on a news release to be reminded when the results were available. With the story in hand, the media would move from latent to aware to active quickly. As an active public, the media were likely to treat the principal's explanation of the test scores as just one of several they quoted, including some that may flat out disagree with the official version.

The neighbors were a nonpublic from the beginning. They were completely unaware of the testing of the children. They would probably remain a nonpublic, even after the media coverage of the test scores. Most would not bother to pay attention to the news reports. Those that did, unless they had a child in the school or a connection to the issue, would probably quickly forget about the matter because (a) it did not involve them, (b) they did not recognize the testing results as a serious issue, and (c) they did not think there was anything they could do about student test scores anyway.

Figure 1.3   Different issues and problems will sort stakeholders into different publics.

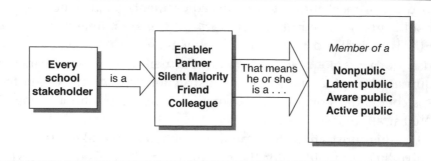

To be effective communication managers, principals have to real-ize that on any given school issue or problem, some stakeholders are latent publics, others are aware publics, and still others are active publics, and each requires him or her to use different communication techniques. In addition, nonpublics can quickly transform into aware or active publics.

Although different publics are going to form in response to differ-ent issues or problems, there are some generalizations about which kinds of publics are likely to form in each stakeholder group. For example, Enablers are at least aware publics and probably active when it comes to most issues. Partners are like Enablers in that most of them are at least aware publics, and many of them are active publics when it comes to most, if not all, of the school's issues and problems.

The only two stakeholder groups with latent publics or nonpub-lic in their ranks are the Silent Majority and Friends. What this means is that when principals initiate communication, they can probably put stakeholders in both of these large categories at the bot-tom of their priority lists. That is not to say there are not important people within these categories who should hear from the principals. There are. But everyone in the other categories is a "must contact" individual. If they do not hear from the principal, they will seek information from someone else, and the principal will struggle to catch up as a credible source of information about the issue. Mean-while, if everyone in the last two stakeholder categories receives the information a day or two later, most will not even notice, and far fewer will care.

Finally, although these generalizations provide principals with some seat-of-the pants guidance, the day-to-day issues will provide all kinds of complicating exceptions. For example, some teachers at a school in a small community have decided to do something about what they perceive as poor-quality professional development sessions. Fed up with 1-day events they say provide limited information on topics with little relevance to their classrooms, they have petitioned the principal and the superintendent for control over the content and delivery of future sessions. This group of teachers is an active public. But other teachers who participate in the same training sessions do not see any problems with them. They are a latent public because they face the same situation, but they do not recognize it as problematic. A third group of teachers are an aware public. Although they also think the sessions are of poor quality, they are not motivated to take any action because some are near retirement and others are planning to transfer schools.

Although all the teachers are members of the Partners stakeholder group, and Partners are generally active publics, on this issue they formed three different publics—active, latent, and aware. Thus, although principals will generalize about the communication behavior of entire stakeholder groups, they need to be cautious about relying on membership in a stakeholder group as a sole predictor of the likely communication behavior of its members. There will always be exceptions, unique cases, and variations.

Summary

This chapter discussed the need for two-way communication between principals and stakeholders. It also introduced readers to the notions of educational stakeholders and key publics. Stakeholders are broad groups of individuals with similar characteristics who have a stake in the school. Some, in fact, are formally tied to the school (Enablers and Partners). Still others are individuals from whom the principal can seek advice and feedback (Friends). Most fall into a Silent Majority category that contains a cross-section of individuals, some of whom have ties to the school and some do not. Stakeholders fall into large categories, and not every person within a particular category is equally interested in an issue or problem facing the school. The degree of interest or involvement an individual has with the school regarding a problem determines his or her placement within a public.

Publics vary in that some have no interest in the school's issues or problems and they are a nonpublic. As such, communicating with them is a lower priority. A latent public is one that just does not know about a school issue or problem and needs to be informed. An aware public is one that recognizes the problem or issue but for a variety of reasons has not yet organized to take any action on it. This is a key audience for the principal because, if ignored, it could easily become an active public on its own and bypass the principal in its information-seeking behavior. If a latent public goes out on its own to satisfy its need for information and does not rely on the principal, that is probably not in the school's best interests. In contrast, an active public has not only recognized the problem or issue but also discussed it, talked among itself about doing something about it, and mobilized to communicate in some way about it. By the time a public is active, it does the principal little good to communicate with it; the public has its mind pretty much made up. This is okay, of course, if the active public is already supportive of the school. It can be disastrous if it formed without the principal's involvement. A principal who is a leader of the active publics within the school's stakeholder groups probably has the communication management under control.

Among the school's stakeholders, aware and active publics dominate among the Enablers and Partners. This suggests that these are all high-priority targets for the principal's communication efforts. The Silent Majority, however, contains many stakeholders with whom the principal would like to be in regular communication but will find it difficult because they belong to latent publics. Finally, on some issues, stakeholders may split and form different publics.

2

Engaging Stakeholders in Meaningful Communications

School leaders using communication management effectively will find it helpful to have a theory base to fall back on when applying what they know to real-world challenges. The best theory for communication management, however, does not come from educational administration; it comes from the study of public relations. Educational administrators may find this disarming because they tend to avoid "public relations" for fear the term smacks of unsavory practices. It is unfortunate that so many school leaders automatically cringe when public relations is included in their management portfolio. Perhaps a simple definition will help make the term more palatable: "Public relations is the management of communication between an organization and its publics" (Grunig & Hunt, 1984, p. 6). By now, readers will have come to realize that is exactly what this book is about. How do school leaders manage the communication between their schools and their stakeholders?

In prior years, school principals were taught in educational administration programs about the need to develop their personal communication skills. The emphasis was on learning how to lead meetings; interact with staff, parents, and community groups; and, in particular, face hostile audiences concerned about the school. To be sure, any good leader needs personal communication skills. Also, all leaders want to be sure that their messages are being conveyed. These skills, however, are insufficient for the school leaders who intend to use communication management methods to gain and hold the trust and respect of their stakeholders, to operate a transparent school, and to carry out the administrative responsibilities of a midlevel district employee simultaneously.

Any search for a theory of communication management will eventually lead to the social sciences and, in particular, the young field of public relations. It was not until the mid-1950s that those who studied public relations defined its purpose: "either to change or neutralize hostile opinions, to crystallize unformed or latent opinions in your favor, or to conserve favorable opinions" (Cutlip & Center, 1958, p. 59). Other researchers agreed, defining public relations as the art and science of informing, influencing, changing, or neutralizing public opinion. Not everyone agreed, however. It became obvious to some social scientists that few public relations practitioners understood the nature of "publics" or knew what "public opinion" was all about. Grunig (1992) noted,

> Although *public relations* is probably the oldest concept used to describe the communication activities of organizations, many organizations now use such terms as *business communication* and *public affairs* to describe these activities—in part because of the negative connotations of public relations. (p. 4)

The concept of public opinion had been studied for some time, but with the advent of survey research in the 1930s, it became difficult to measure the opinions of the many publics. Thus, the concept of public opinion evolved into mass opinion.

The populist notion that most people have opinions on most issues persists in the minds of many public relations practitioners today and especially in the minds of their client organizations. Thus, public relations is practiced with the idea that its practitioners can influence mass opinion on behalf of clients or hope that if they "get their message out" mass opinion will support them (Grunig, 1997, p. 5). Grunig quoted Richard Harwood, writing in the *Washington*

Post, who explored the folly of this particular belief system by pointing out contradictions in polls of the general population:

> Harwood produced a poll where about two thirds of the people interviewed in the United States, Canada, Britain, and France thought that "things were going badly in their countries." At the same time, polls showed that 85% of the people in the United States "were quite satisfied with the way things were going in their own lives; nearly 70% said things were going well in their own communities." (p. 5)

Harwood concluded his article by saying, "It is fair to say that 'public opinion' exists very spottily in this country—if it exists at all—and that 'well-informed' public opinion is even scarcer." Grunig added,

> If we return to the classic theories of publics, such results are to be expected and can be explained easily. Humans simply do not have the time or the ability to be concerned about every problem in the world. They devote their time and energy to the problems that involve them and for which they can make a difference. (p. 6)

That sentence bears repeating. Paraphrased, it makes a statement that new school principals should consider writing down and pasting onto the back of their office doors in large letters:

> My school's stakeholders simply do not have the time or the ability to be concerned about all my school's issues and problems. They only devote their time and energy to those that involve them, and for which they believe they can influence or impact.

This statement should provide principals with a good deal of relief and considerable concern at the same time. One the one hand, many things principals may think are troublesome issues are not going to register as problems with most of their schools' stakeholders. Conversely, occasionally principals will have to deal with issues that will need the involvement of some of their key stakeholders and principals will be hard-pressed to get their attention.

Principals need to be concerned about publics that have an involvement with the school, recognize the school's problems, and believe that they have the ability to help address them. These are the primary publics that are bound to arise in any given situation.

Using the Theory to Make Sense of Communication Management

Publics that develop around problems or issues differ in the extent to which they are aware of the problem and can do something about it. These are explored in Grunig's (1997, p. 10) "situational theory" of communication behavior and its three independent variables:

> Problem recognition: People detect that something should be done about a situation and stop to think about what to do.

> Constraint recognition: People perceive that there are obstacles in a situation that limit their ability to do anything about it.

> Level of involvement: This is the extent to which people connect themselves with a situation.

Problem Recognition

> The basic idea behind the concept of problem recognition is that people do not stop to think about a situation unless they perceive that something needs to be done to improve the situation. When they detect such a problem, they do most of their communicating because they need information to help solve it.
>
> —Grunig and Hunt (1984, p. 149)

For example, if the principal announces year after year that enrollment is increasing, it is unlikely that many of his stakeholders are going to sense a problem. Growing enrollment seems perfectly natural. If the enrollment data are pared to a "maximum capacity" figure that has long been exceeded, pictures of overcrowded classrooms, or modules constructed on the playgrounds, however, the news of more students takes on a whole new meaning. All of a sudden, there is "problem recognition."

Constraint Recognition

Constraint recognition represents the extent to which people perceive that there are constraints—or obstacles—in a situation that limit their freedom to plan their own behavior. If people do not think they can do something about a situation, just knowing about it is not sufficient to get them to seek information about it or process information about it. Principals frequently deal with this problem when confronting parents from immigrant families. They very much want their children to receive a quality education, but they frequently are reluctant to get involved in parent education initiatives because of a language barrier or their heavy work schedules. They feel "constrained" and thus probably do not pay much attention to the onslaught of communication from the school. If principals want these parents to be more involved in the school's activities, they are going to have to first address the constraints. For this reason, principals will have to work around the parents' work schedules and provide for a bilingual parental aide, even if it is inconvenient for the teachers.

Level of Involvement

The third independent variable, level of involvement, helps to distinguish whether the person's communication behavior will be active or passive. A member of a public who perceives a strong involvement in an issue generally also has high problem recognition and low constraint recognition for that issue. As a result, an involved public usually will be the most active public. It will seek and process information and use that information to develop ideas, attitudes, and behaviors (Grunig & Hunt, 1984, p. 152).

Principals know that the first step in getting parents involved with the school is to get them to attend a back-to-school night. If they show up for that, then maybe they will sign up for the PTA/PTO. If they join the PTA/PTO, they are likely to become candidates for a volunteer group of one sort or another. Once they volunteer for something, they will undoubtedly volunteer for something else. Then they are hooked. (See Chapter 5 for an excellent example of this strategy played out in one of the case studies.) Once they are involved, they will stay involved as long as they have children in the school.

If people have high involvement with an issue, they also tend to have high problem recognition. Common sense suggests it would be difficult to be affected by something an organization does without seeing that consequence as a problem. High involvement also decreases constraint recognition because involved people generally try to remove constraints that otherwise would discourage them from communicating and doing something about the problem. For this reason, most principals would quickly recognize members of the school board with children enrolled in their school, as well as parents who serve as officers in their PTA/PTO and as members of their school advisory committees, as active publics. They have high involvement, high problem recognition, and low constraint (Table 2.1). Based on

Table 2.1   General Behavior of Publics According to Situation Variables

The Resulting Type of Public Formed Is . . .	If Problem Recognition Is . . .	and Constraint Recognition Is . . .	and Level of Involvement Is . . .	Information Seeking or Processing Behavior Is . . .
Active	High	Low	High	Reinforcing; has made a decision about the situation and moved into an action mode of behavior
Aware	Low/high	Low/high	High	Actively seeking information from all sources
Latent	Low	Low	High	Processing, but not necessarily retaining anything
Nonpublic	Low	High	Low	Nonexistent

Grunig's research, Table 2.1 summarizes the four types of publics that tend to form and the degree of information seeking/processing that usually results from the most common combinations of variables.

Grunig's situational theory has proven invaluable to public relations professionals because it provides concrete indicators about the probable behavior of stakeholders when confronted with a problem or issue. Four patterns of stakeholder behavior should be noted (Grunig & Hunt, 1984):

> Publics that are active on most issues: This type of public forms essentially as an activist public composed of stakeholders who seek to challenge organizations on many different issues.

> Publics that are active on a single issue: This type of public forms because the stakeholders are interested in one issue only; they pursue that issue while ignoring other issues.

> Publics that are active only on issues that involve nearly everyone: This type of public forms only when stakeholders perceive

themselves to be part of a larger group that has an interest in the outcome of an issue.

Publics that are apathetic on all issues: This type of public forms from stakeholders who remain inactive on nearly all issues.

Passively communicating publics will not go out of their way to obtain information, but they may process information if it comes to them, assuming it does not require any effort on their part to get the information.

Publics that simply process information, rather than seek it, often remain latent publics. Sometimes, they become aware publics, but they seldom become active publics (Grunig & Hunt, 1984, p. 151). This is important for principals to remember. They can bombard people with information, but if the members of the public are passive, most of them will not remember the contents of the information soon after receiving it.

What increases the likelihood that members of a public will both seek and process information, of course, is the degree to which they recognize the problem as having some relevance to them. If they recognize something as a problem, stakeholders are more likely to process information they receive about it and to seek information about it. Also, because they recognize the problem, the information they obtain will be remembered and have an effect.

Sorting Out Likely Communication Behavior of Publics

As Table 2.1 illustrates, situational theory can become complex. It would be unrealistic to expect busy principals to keep four different kinds of publics in mind when they are managing communications along with a host of other duties. Fortunately, some of the publics occur much more often than others. This is because the three independent variables—problem recognition, constraint recognition, and level of involvement—affect each other. A principal can reduce the number of publics quickly by first determining people's likely involvement (high or low). This will enable the principal to determine their likely problem recognition and constraint recognition. High involvement generally means high problem recognition and low constraint.

The situational theory helps considerably by suggesting the probable communication behavior of a public when confronted with a problem or issue. Numerous communication studies involving all

Figure 2.1   Principals learn that their communication behavior must be different with stakeholder publics who are active on all issues than it is with those who are apathetic on all issues or active on only certain issues.

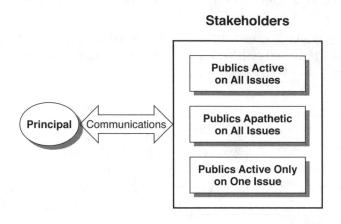

kinds of people in all kinds of situations show that although the probability that people will engage in some kind of communication behavior is relatively low, their willingness to engage differs substantially among various publics. A regular pattern of communication behavior among publics emerges from the studies, with three (by collapsing the two single-issue publics into one) types dominating (Fig. 2.1).

The following guidelines can maximize the effectiveness of school communications:

1. Find ways to help stakeholders become part of active publics in support of their schools.

In today's environment, principals need to involve as many stakeholders as possible in support of their schools. When an issue arises, it is critical to transform stakeholders into active or aware publics that have a high probability of seeking information and engaging in actions that positively impact the school. Unfortunately, it can be enormously challenging for principals to alter the stance of latent publics and nonpublics, which typically are larger than active and aware publics.

However, Grunig's (1992, p. 137) research found that the degree of involvement plays a key role in predicting the likelihood that stakeholders will become connected and personally vested in issues. Grunig discovered that a stakeholder's level of involvement is actually the key variable that can affect the other variables. High involvement generally leads to high problem recognition and low constraint recognition, both of which help stakeholders to become part of an active or aware public. Thus, to effect changes in a school, principals can accomplish much by boosting involvement.

This explains why getting parents to attend back-to-school nights and other events has a potentially high payoff. If parents attend a school function, they may sign up for the PTA/PTO. If they join the PTA/PTO, they are more likely to participate in a school committee of one sort or another. Once they volunteer for something, they will probably volunteer for something else if they have a positive experience. This spiraling level of involvement is what eventually leads to fashioning active or aware publics around the school.

High involvement also leads to higher levels of information seeking and processing. The more stakeholders are involved in the school, the more likely they are to seek or process information, and, therefore, the more principals need to communicate with them. When publics receive communications that help them understand an organization, they are more willing to support it.

It is also important to note that communicating with a public can lead to unintended reactions. For example, a public may disagree with the organization after receiving a communication about an issue. If the neighbors do not know the school is going to install portable classrooms, they are unlikely to be upset about it. Tell them the news, and they are likely to be upset. This is always a risk in communicating. Principals who conclude that the risk is too great to warrant communicating in the first place, however, are more likely to lose their public than those who accept the risk and communicate openly.

2. When working with an active public on a difficult issue or a crisis, communicate proactively.

It is best for principals to communicate openly and frequently with members of an active public because these stakeholders not only process information but also tend to seek more of it. When a serious problem or crisis occurs, these stakeholders are likely to expect and demand that the principal, as the school leader, be honest and forthcoming with any necessary information. If they believe a principal is not communicating sufficiently, they will search for other sources for information. This can lead to conflict, especially if the other sources of information offer an explanation that contradicts that of the principal. Taking the approach of "battening down the hatches" until the storm is over is precisely the wrong strategy.

3. When communicating with a latent public whose members are low on information processing and seeking, it is important to develop a unique communication strategy that will attract them to the messages.

An active public helps communicators get their messages across because its members search for information and try to understand it when they obtain it. Members of a latent public, however, typically do not look for information and generally will put forth little effort to understand the information when it comes to them. As a result, messages intended for this type of public should be brief and straightforward, with a higher level of attention given to style and creativity.

Principals should avoid mailing out lengthy letters and memos, or items that look like unsolicited mail, because members of a latent public may read them with only a cursory glance, retaining little. It is far more effective to send short, clear, and convincing messages that simply convey the idea, "Here's an issue or problem, and it involves you." Such a communication should include a note about how to obtain more information from a particular person at the school or the school's Web site.

4. When it is important to communicate with a nonpublic or a latent public with low involvement and low problem recognition (whose stakeholders can have an impact on your organization), it may be possible to reach them through information processing.

Although members of such a public do not generally seek information or allow communication to have an effect on them, it can be worthwhile to try to connect with at least some members through information processing. Their involvement may then stimulate problem recognition, prompting other members of that public to seek additional information and become aware or active.

5. When dealing with an issue or problem that will likely engender low involvement and low problem recognition, sometimes it is best to conclude that communicating about it is not worth the time and money because the issue has a low probability of enticing a public to listen or act.

Although this may seem uncaring, it is a real-politick stance that principals must consider. The fact is that some issues simply do not inspire a public to sense that a problem exists, so few stakeholders will be concerned enough to do anything about the issue. An example is declining attendance at the sophomore class's annual variety show. Communicating about this issue may not be the best use of time, effort, and money compared to targeting communication with regard to issues that affect larger numbers of stakeholders.

Communicating with someone who may not like the message is always a danger and frequently sufficiently scary to warrant not communicating in the first place. Many school administrators have kept their mouths shut for fear of saying something that would upset their stakeholders. Unfortunately, they have been conditioned to think this is always good advice. Of course, they need to be reminded that if they do not communicate, they can hardly expect their untold story to win them many endorsements, particularly when others are actively communicating their interpretation of what is going on at their school. No communication, or the hackneyed "no response" comment, will generate hostility toward the school and add one more item to the list of things the critics find wrong with its leadership.

Summary

In this chapter, school leaders learned it is not sufficient to just know who the school's stakeholders are. When an issue or problem arises, it will create a corresponding public or publics within the stakeholders. These publics will vary, depending on whether they (a) face the problem or issue, (b) recognize that it exists, and (c) are organizing to do something about it. In some cases, an issue will create all three audiences across the stakeholders. Studies of organizations, however, suggest that publics tend to fall into three general categories: publics that are active on all the issues, publics that are apathetic on all issues, and publics that are active only on single issues. Finally, research has produced five implications for school principals that will be further explored in Chapter 4.

3

Four Approaches to Communication Management

So far, this book has introduced the reader to stakeholders and emphasized the importance of having a strong working relationship with the school's "partners"—the school employees, students, family members, and community groups most closely connected to the school. The principal knows that with each issue or problem that arises, there will be different "publics" that form in reaction to it. They will range from "latent" publics to "active" publics, depending on the extent to which stakeholders recognize the problem, believe it involves them, think there are any constraints that limit their ability to do anything about it, and, finally, organize with others to do something about it.

So far so good. All of that is just interesting background reading, however. Simply knowing about it will not help new principals become effective school leaders. What will make a difference is what they learn to do as a consequence of their knowledge about publics. This is what makes up the content of this chapter. In other words, this chapter is the mother lode of the book. It is the tap root of what principals need to know about communication management. In short, this chapter requires principals to stick with a discussion of the two-way symmetric model long enough to master it. When they do, they will be rewarded with something called the "mixed-motive" model of communication management. This is the communication management model every principal needs to master. It is not something school administrators will learn in an educational administration course, but it may well be the key to their survival as a practicing school administrator.

Learning the Four Basic Communication Models

There are basically four common types of communication models that all organizations use. Schools are no strangers to any of them. For example, schools still occasionally fall back on the oldest of the models, the "press agentry/publicity" model. Acting as their own press agents, principals will attempt to pack their auditoriums for a back-to-school event employing some of P. T. Barnum's ploys, including bells and whistles if they have them. The stakeholders who receive this material expect nothing less and would be disappointed if they got anything different.

Sometimes, a principal wants to know what a critical stakeholder public is thinking before communicating with it about an issue. Thus, the principal will formally or informally assess its views on the topic. Then, he will revise his communication accordingly to bring it in line with the views of his intended audience. This is using a "two-way asymmetric" model of communication.

Most of the time, however, school principals engage in the "public information" model. This model has them distributing newsworthy information about the school to stakeholders on a routine basis. When schools are most bureaucratic, they generally practice the safe public information model. It is difficult to criticize the school principal for passing on information in a journalistic manner: It is the best information available, it is truthful, and it has been approved by the principal's superiors as suitable for sharing. No principal will get into serious trouble for practicing the public information model of public relations. No principal will ever be judged a leader by her school, community, and family partnership, however, if all the information she is able to share with them comes through a school newsletter. Such information is one way—from the organization to the stakeholders. It is the organization telling the stakeholders what the organization wants them to know and consequently to accept. That is not leadership: That is old-fashioned manipulation. It is bureaucratic, and it is ineffective. The smart principal knows it and realizes that he has to listen to his stakeholders as well as talk to them. He has to understand their points of view if he hopes to get them to understand his. This form of communication is called the "two-way symmetric" model of communication management.

All four models of communication have utility for public schools; what the principal needs to learn, however, is that some have much more currency than others. Also, the one that may be most beneficial is not even among the four.

Press Agentry/Publicity Model

Publicists probably have been peddling their puffery for as long as there has been a press to print it. Certainly, as a profession, they have had a colorful past. Probably none among them is better known than Phineas T. Barnum, the founder of the Barnum and Bailey Circus. The saying, "There's no such thing as bad publicity," is associated with Barnum, as is the whole notion of the publicist/press agent model of public relations. The fact that Barnum was not overly concerned about the truth was perhaps best captured in his immortal line, "There's a sucker born every minute."

Press agents were not hoodwinking the public just to sell comics and promote circuses. Major corporations hired them to promote their products and attack their critics. Few companies in the early 1900s, however, thought it important to explain themselves to the public, let alone allow the public to have a say in the way they were managed. Another famous phrase from this era, "The public be damned," is believed to have originated from the president of New York Central Railroad when asked why he did not maintain a train that the public wanted (Bernays, 1952, pp. 51–52). Although nobody is sure if the quote is accurate, historians are comfortable asserting that it did reflect a prevailing philosophy of corporate America at the time.

Eventually, the excesses of "Big Business" created a backlash. A group of "muckrakers," such as Lincoln Steffens and Upton Sinclair, found an outlet for their writing in several popular magazines of the day. The corruption of the corporations was being exposed almost faster than the press agents could cover it up.

At approximately the same time, a journalist who freelanced as a publicist had a novel idea. Writing in a New York newspaper, Ivy Lee said that if a corporation was concerned about its reputation, it should tell the truth about its actions. Lee said a company—he could just have well been talking about a public school—should tell the truth, and if that truth was damaging to the organization, then the organization should change its behavior so the truth could be told without fear (Grunig & Hunt, 1984, p. 31). This rather straightforward piece of advice would result in generations of public relations students being required to memorize his name and to remember him as one of the first practitioners of the public information model.

Today, the press agent/publicity model is out of favor except among organizations that want to get attention in the media for themselves or their clients. Good examples are professional sports, movie and television agents, politicians, and anyone with a product to sell.

Public Information Model

The American Telephone & Telegraph Company (AT&T), finding its public image low, was the first company in the United States to hire a public relations firm. The Boston-based company was called the Publicity Bureau, and it was the nation's first public relations firm. By 1923, the public relations function at AT&T had been institutionalized. The head of its public relations department stated the company's philosophy in terms that clearly fit the public information model (N. L. Griese as quoted in Grunig & Hunt, 1984):

> All business in a democratic country begins with public permission and exists by public approval. If that be true, it follows that business should be cheerfully willing to tell the public what its policies are, what it is doing, and what it hopes to do. That seems practically a duty. (p. 36)

At approximately the same time, major nonprofits came into being, and they also chose to operate with this philosophy. Soon, "journalists in residence" became the norm in corporations, trade associations, nonprofits, government agencies, and school districts. The "press agent" model was all but gone, replaced by the "public information" model. Civic-minded organizations were determined to provide their stakeholders with "information" and not "public relations."

The public information model came into vogue after World War I and has remained the most popular of the models ever since.

Two-Way Asymmetric Model

During World War I, the U.S. government mounted a massive propaganda effort to build support for the war effort. When the war ended, it left in its wake a group of well-trained practitioners, several of whom drifted into universities to become the first serious scholars in the field of public relations. One of them, Edward L. Bernays, taught the first university course on public relations and wrote the first book on the topic. He is mentioned here not so much for that fact but because he was a disciple of Ivy Lee and his belief in the notion that organizations should be transparent, tell the truth about themselves, and change their behavior when they are wrong.

The notion of "transparency" is not new, as Lee instructs us, but the concept remains controversial to this day. That is, not everyone is in favor of it. The Freedom of Information Act would not have been necessary if government agencies believed in transparent governance. It is not uncommon for government agencies and corporations that do business with them to grumble about "the transparency problem" that arises from the need to disclose their dealings to the public (Henry, 2004, p. E1).

Another novel idea that has been around for a long time, but still not totally embraced by organizations today, is the concept of doing what the public expects one to do. Normally, public relations is concerned with explaining management's views to the public. Bernays demonstrated to management, however, that it was good business to determine what values and attitudes publics had and then describe the organization in a way that conformed to those values and attitudes. For example, if the community wants a company to be "safe and reliable," then the company would make a point of selling itself as safe and reliable. This is called the two-way asymmetric model.

Here is how it works. Consider a situation in which two neighboring high schools have to merge because of declining enrollments. Before announcing the closure, the principals get together and discuss how to announce the news. They know there will be many upset stakeholders. Therefore, they conduct a survey, which reveals that one positive aspect of a merger recognized by many stakeholders is the prospect of better athletic teams emerging from the combined student bodies. Consequently, when announcing the merger, the two principals play up the positive aspects of the strengthened athletics that the new school will be able to muster. By so doing, the principals are able to rally support for at least this positive spin of the merger while downplaying the negative aspects. They were able to do this because they practiced the two-way asymmetric model of communication whereby they first found out what their publics wanted and then told them this is what they were providing.

Generally, when an organization employs this model, it conducts studies to determine what stakeholders like about the organization and then publicizes those findings, or the organization will (Grunig &

Hunt, 1984) determine what values and attitudes publics have and then describe the organization in a way that conforms to these values and attitudes. Bernays called these strategies the "crystallizing of public opinion" and the "engineering of consent" (p. 40).

Two-Way Symmetric Model

Historians claim that most of the early public relations pioneers understood the need for the two-way symmetric model, even if they did not practice it. One of the earlier practitioners said, "It is just as important for company management to understand the problems and viewpoints of its employees, neighbors, and others as it is for these groups to understand the problems and viewpoints of management" (Hill, 1963, p. 6). Ivy Lee (as quoted in Grunig & Hunt, 1984) reportedly told the Rockefellers to tell the truth "because sooner or later the public will find it out anyway. And if the public doesn't like what you are doing, change your policies and bring them into line with what the people want" (p. 42).

Basically, in the two-way symmetric model, organizations and their publics together address an issue that impacts them both, use dispute-resolution techniques to negotiate mutually beneficial outcomes, and work together to come to a "win-win" position.

In an educational context, a principal using the two-way symmetric model would clearly be exhibiting the characteristics of interactional administrative leadership. By that, we mean the principal would be highly focused on fostering productive social relations among teachers as well as parents and others involved with the school. In such a cooperative social system, principals are the leaders, but they are primarily group members, and their actions on behalf of the group are validated by it. In such a relationship, individuals have different degrees of relative power, with the principal having the most. Each must necessarily reach accommodation with the other to serve their mutual interests, however.

Group members—in the school's case, this would probably be the partnership or a subset of the Partners—constantly bargain and negotiate a mix of benefits and costs among themselves and between themselves and the principal. Teachers, parents, and other community organizations are all doing a constant analysis of that which can be gained and that which must be expended to achieve that gain. Benefits and costs are defined according to individual and collective normative frameworks. These frameworks incorporate beliefs and assumptions regarding self-interests, the interests of others, goals, and rewards, as well as beliefs and assumptions regarding roles, responsibilities, rights, and obligations in their relationships with their neighborhood school. Sometimes everything clicks; sometimes it does not.

Another way of thinking about the use of the two-way symmetric model is when a principal introduces a school, family, and community partnership. It would be nearly impossible to operate such a partnership using any other communication model. At their very core are the notions of respect and trust. What creates these, of course, is communication. Top-down, one-way communication, even if it is honest and reliable, is not going to create the environment necessary for a successful partnership to flourish. It requires two-way communication in which the principal is willing to listen, negotiate, and compromise on occasion.

Goodwin (2004) noted that as the role of principals changes,

> they are beginning to realize they need to interact with people in the school, the district, and the community and the interaction involves social changes as well as school expectations, politics and bureaucracy as well as daily school life, and standards and accountability as well as the social and emotional needs of students. (p. 17)

The old "command-and-control" management style is on the way out. Principals are expected to operate "transparent" schools. The move to an autonomous management system in which the principal has increased authority and power independent of a central office has not replaced it yet, however. Consequently, many principals will feel caught between conflicting systems and wonder which communication management approach to use as they sort it out.

Which Model Works Best?

Of course, the question that has intrigued organizational theorists and managers alike for decades is, Which model is the best? The answer is, "No one approach is appropriate all the time for all conditions."

If a principal is trying to sell tickets to a school bazaar, then the press agentry/publicity model is the most appropriate. If the principal is simply disseminating information about the school bus schedule for the coming year, the public information model will work fine. Consider a principal who has been asked by the senior class to sponsor an all-night party on their graduation night, however. The principal thinks the idea has merit, but he's not sure the parents will go along with the idea. Therefore, before he announces the event, he conducts a survey. He asks the parents of the seniors what their greatest

Table 3.1   Characteristics of Four Communication Models

Characteristic	Press Agentry/ Publicity	Public Information	Two-Way Asymmetric	Two-Way Symmetric
Purpose	Propaganda	Dissemination of information	Scientific persuasion	Mutual understanding
Nature of communication	One-way	One-way	Two-way	Two-way
Where practiced	Sports, theater promotions	Government agencies, nonprofits	Competitive businesses	Regulated businesses

fear is about what the seniors might do the night after they receive their high school diplomas. Armed with their worst stories as evidence, he could then announce that the seniors had come up with the perfect solution: They had agreed to lock themselves in a room all night and listen to music rather than get into cars and expose themselves to alcohol and other temptations that the open road might offer. That is using the two-way asymmetric model to get the school and the public aligned.

Finally, if principals are serious about involving parents and community members as partners in the operation of the school, they will demonstrate it by using the two-way symmetric model, which requires give-and-take communication.

As Table 3.1 depicts, each of the four models has a different purpose. The three-nation study of organizations conducted by Grunig and colleagues in 1990–1991 revealed that organizations tend to use all four models, although the public information model is the overwhelming favorite, and the two-way symmetric model is the least used. Interestingly, the researchers found a major difference between "excellent" and "less-than-excellent" organizations. That is, "excellent organizations were more apt to use both types of advanced practices, including the two-way asymmetric model, which emphasizes persuasion, and the two-way symmetric model, which emphasizes mutual understanding and dispute resolution" (Dozier, 1995, p. 216). The explanation for the mixed use makes sense, however. That is, the organizations particularly relied on the two-way symmetric model for employees and community communication (pp. 214–215). It would stand to reason that the kinds of organizations studied—excellent businesses, nonprofits, and government agencies—would be enlightened enough about employee and community relations to practice the two-way symmetric model. By the same token, they used the two-way asymmetric model to learn more about their publics' views so that the managers were in a better position to align their corporate interests with the expressed interests of the publics.

The use of the two-way asymmetric model is clearly designed to achieve some short-term advantage for the organization. An excellent organization's use of any of the asymmetric models, however, has to be tempered by its core philosophy to ensure that short-term tactical advantages do not jeopardize the organization's long-term strategy being nurtured by the use of the two-way symmetric communication model.

If we were to extrapolate what the social scientists learned from their study to a typical school district, we would depict it as shown in Figure 3.1. That is, the district attempts to use the asymmetric model to promote its position on an issue to the stakeholders. The stakeholders, in turn, use asymmetric models to promote their positions on issues to the district. Both the district and the stakeholders, however, would rely on the symmetrical communication model to ensure that the basis for their relationship remains harmonious and governed by mutual respect and trust.

Figure 3.1   Principals will use an asymmetric model of communication when they want to convince stakeholders to adopt the district's way of thinking. Likewise, the stakeholders can use this model to convince the district to adopt the views of the parents, students, teachers, and community. A symmetric model enables both the principals and their stakeholders to communicate with one another to reach agreement on issues and problems.

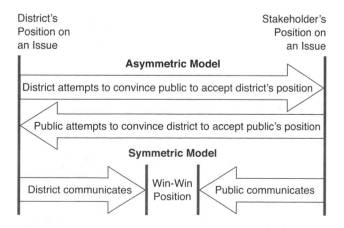

Different Kinds of Companies, Different Communication Models

Historically, public schools managed their communication efforts much like corporations did. That is, for the most part, school districts and individual schools employed a version of the public information model. Principals generally believed they were being responsible when they convinced their stakeholders to do something principals thought was to the stakeholders' benefit.

Today, many public school stakeholders have made it clear that they no longer want to be recipients of that kind of benevolence. The issue is not just a matter of trust. Principals are much more likely today to distribute leadership responsibilities among their staff, to involve the community in the school's operation, and to view the Parents as active Partners in their children's education. Principals who operate transparent schools, who believe the Enablers and the Partners are all players, practice two-way symmetric communication.

Organizations that employ two-way symmetric communication are definitely different than organizations that rely on the asymmetric models (publicity/press agentry, public information, and one-way asymmetric). This became apparent from the major three-nation study mentioned previously (the Excellence Study conducted by Grunig and colleagues) of the working practices of corporations, associations, and government agencies. The researchers found that companies tended to have different organizational characteristics depending on which of the communication management models they employed.

For example, organizations that use the asymmetric models (publicity, public information, and two-way asymmetric) tend to be characterized by the following:

- Internal orientation: Members of the organization look out from the organization and do not see the organization as outsiders see it.
- Closed system: Information flows out from the organization and not into it.
- Elitism: Leaders of the organization know best. They have more knowledge than members of publics. Wisdom is not a product of a "free marketplace of ideas."
- Conservation: Change is undesirable. Outside efforts to change the organization should be resisted; pressure for change should be considered subversive.

- Tradition: Tradition provides an organization with stability and helps it to maintain its culture.
- Central authority: Power should be concentrated in the hands of a few top managers. Employees should have little autonomy. Organizations should be managed as autocracies (Grunig, 1989, pp. 17–44).

Although this list of organizational characteristics did not originate from public schools, it certainly could have. Public schools have a long and storied history of adopting many of the less flattering features of their corporate counterparts. In other words, overall, the public school system in the United States—throughout most of its history—has had much in common with the less than sterling corporations, government agencies, and associations that social scientists found using the asymmetric models of communication management.

In contrast, organizations that employed the symmetric model (the one that sought mutual understanding between management and publics) typically had the following characteristics:

- Interdependence: Organizations cannot isolate themselves from their environment. Although organizations have boundaries that separate them from their environment, publics and other organizations in their environment "interpenetrate" organizations.
- Open system: The organization is open to interpenetrating systems and freely exchanges information with those systems.
- Moving equilibrium: Organizations as systems strive toward an equilibrium with other systems, an equilibrium state that constantly moves as the environment changes. Systems may attempt to establish equilibrium by controlling other systems; by adapting themselves to other systems; or by making mutual, cooperative adjustments. Their symmetric worldview prefers cooperative and mutual adjustment to control and adaptation.
- Equity: People should be given equal opportunity and be respected as fellow human beings. Anyone, regardless of education or background, may provide valuable input to an organization.
- Autonomy: People are more innovative, constructive, and self-fulfilled when they have the autonomy to influence their own behavior rather than having it controlled by others. Autonomy maximizes employee satisfaction inside the organization and cooperation outside the organization.

- Innovation: New ideas and flexible thinking rather than tradition and efficiency should be stressed.
- Decentralization of management: Management should be collective; managers should coordinate rather than dictate. Decentralization increases autonomy, employee satisfaction, and innovation.
- Responsibility: People and organizations must be concerned with consequences of their behaviors on others and attempt to eliminate adverse consequences.
- Conflict resolution: Conflict should be resolved through negotiation, communication, and compromise and not through force, manipulation, coercion, or violence (Grunig, 1989, pp. 17–44).

Today's much more open, transparent, reform-minded public schools are likely to resemble these organizations and exhibit many of their characteristics. They also are likely to be led by principals who have a core philosophy that embraces the symmetric model of communication management whereby communication is two-way between the school and its publics and is designed to produce a "win-win" for the school.

In their classic text, *The School and Community Relations*, Bagin and Gallagher (2001, p. 13) noted that the two-way symmetric model is the only viable option for the 21st-century school. They stated that there is a need for "systematic, continuous, two-way, honest" communication between the school and its many publics, particularly parents and community members. They concluded,

> Perhaps another way of expressing the same concepts is to say that sound and constructive relations between the school and community are achieved through a process of exchanging information, ideas, and viewpoints out of which common understandings are developed and decisions are made concerning essential improvements in the educational program and adjustments to the climate of social change. (p. 13)

That is the way it should work. In a perfect world, a principal would be fully engaged in a school-family-community partnership and modeling symmetric communication in every situation. Not all principals are going to work in a district that provides them with the opportunity to provide their school with such refreshing and necessary leadership, however. Some school systems, large and small alike, are beset with problems that keep the focus off the principals' need for leadership at the school level. In this case, the principal needs to master the mixed-motive approach to communication management.

Today's Situation Requires a Different Communication Model

Most analysts of the institutional level of schooling (i.e., the "interface of the school with its larger environment") argue that an industrial approach, which led to a "cult of professionalism" in educational administration, dominated throughout the 20th century. The cult of professionalism resulted in "almost complete separation of schools from the community and, in turn, discouragement of local community involvement in decision making related to the administration of schools." It also helped to "marginalize parents as coproducers of their children's learning" (Murphy, 1999, p. 12).

Internally, principals operated as midlevel managers within larger school district organizations. Through most of the 20th century, education modeled its leadership systems on hierarchical, somewhat heroic visions of the school leader—the image of the man in the principal's office (Hart, 1995; Wolcott, 1973). These views of leadership were tied historically to structural, bureaucratic conceptions of schools as organizations (Bacharach & Mundell, 1995; Smylie & Hart, 1999, p. 428).

In essence, children were seen simply as students, families were expected to leave the education of the children to the school, teachers were expected to focus on teaching, and principals were expected to manage the school. Thus, it is not surprising that educational administrators have long been taught to believe that managing communication, for the most part, is all about "building confidence in the schools" among stakeholders (Bagin & Gallagher, 2001, p. 7).

Consequently, many older administrators housed within central offices of school districts, trained in a previous age, might well have different points of views than the new leaders selected to be school principals about how schools should function in the 21st century. Many of those who received their training 20 or more years ago were educated and trained under a different set of assumptions about the role of school leaders.

Today, principals are developing new leadership strategies. A common strategy is "interactional principal leadership," which assumes that even though individuals may enter into a social relationship with different degrees of relative power, each necessarily must reach accommodation with others to serve their mutual interests. Bargaining and negotiation involve a calculus of benefits and costs, an analysis of that which can be gained and that which must be expended to achieve that gain. Benefits and costs are defined according to individual and collective normative frameworks. These frameworks incorporate beliefs and assumptions regarding self-interests, the interests of others, goals, and rewards, as well as beliefs and assumptions regarding roles, responsibilities, rights, and obligations in social relationships (Smylie & Hart, 1999, p. 429; see also Jones, 1983).

The amount of influence, in other words, that modern-day principals have over decisions made at their schools is proportional to their stakeholders' evaluation of their leaders' demonstrated loyalty, competence, and success in helping stakeholders solve their problems and attain their goals. Leaders who demonstrate good judgment and support may accumulate "idiosyncracy credits" from group members. These credits can later be "spent" to achieve a leader's objectives, particularly in difficult or contentious situations (Yukl, 1994; see also Buchanan, 1974; Smylie & Hart, 1999, p. 429).

Today's principals work to foster collective responsibility, mutual trust and obligations, and joint accountability among themselves and their faculty and staff. Although leadership is no longer the principal's sole prerogative now that it is shared, the principal still has the job of creating structures and occasions for interaction to take place and for social bonds to form that enable groups to interact and establish broad support systems.

Principals play an active role in ensuring that everyone gets along and works side by side productively. They foster social relations by demonstrating consistency and competence in their own work. They model commitment, and they repeatedly demonstrate their contributions to the school community. Principals also foster social trust by providing teachers with strong, dependable, and facilitative support. The principals make the improvement of teaching a public and a collective enterprise, they manage conflict fairly and effectively, and they share authority and leadership broadly among teachers.

Principals create joint tasks and multiple-partner efforts to build trust among teachers, parents, students, and community members. They are given opportunities to exchange ideas and information and to form social bonds. They are also encouraged—and funded—to obtain new information from outside the school by bringing in expert consultants or staff developers.

Principals today promote social capital by communicating norms and expectations of community and teamwork. These are the focal points around which social relations can form, function, and grow. Once principals have strong social capital, they can enforce the norms and expectations that built it by holding the teachers, parents, and students individually accountable for their actions and by promoting collective mechanisms of accountability and collegial control.

Principals with strong social capital among key stakeholders can work to develop social relations within their schools and create enough closure of the social group to sustain its strength and cohesiveness. At the same time, these principals are able to recognize the importance of establishing relations with community groups and others to evoke new information, challenges, and perspectives that will have meaning and contribute to the improvement of their schools. This is all done for good reason: "The research suggests that an appropriate balance between internal and external ties is most conducive to learning and improvement" (Smylie & Hart, 1999, pp. 436–437).

Principals who need to function within school districts but lead progressive school partnerships need a new communication model.

When a Principal Has to Placate Two Critical Publics

Ideally, school principals would operate in complete harmony with their Partners and their Enablers. Everybody would be on the same page and in complete agreement about goals and objectives for the students and the schools. Fortunately, for most of the goals and objectives, this is the case. Year in and year out, however, there are going to be tensions. For example, the federal No Child Left Behind Act of 2001 puts districts under considerable pressure to raise student test scores. This pressure frequently results in school districts putting much more emphasis on those subjects that will be tested.

The school day only has so many hours, of course, so if more time is going to be spent on math and reading instruction, then time spent on other disciplines must be reduced. Consequently, schools throughout the country have been reducing the time they spend teaching arts and music or allowing students onto the playground for recess. These decisions have created backlashes at schools from various Partners who argue that children are losing their opportunity to develop a fine arts appreciation and who worry about child obesity.

Conflicts between Enablers and Partners test the principals' communication management skills. That is, principals may well agree with their Partners that the curriculum the school offered was appropriate to the student body before the passage of No Child Left Behind. The law is not something the community can ignore, however. As administrators in the district, the principals have to carry out the mandate as it is passed down to them from the federal government through the state departments of education and their own district offices. Therefore, the principals have little choice but to attempt to continue operating transparent schools with shared management and two-way communication systems in which negotiation and compromise are the norm. At the same time, however, they have to employ the extremely bureaucratic top-down, one-way communication model that instructs them how the school will operate according to the new federal mandate. Switching communication models—the so-called mixed-motives approach to communication—likely will be challenged by the principals' Partners and cause dissention within their partnerships. It certainly will test their leadership skills.

No Single Communication Strategy Works All the Time

When the social scientists who conducted the three-nation study of communication behavior within organizations focused on the very best, they found that even the top-of-the-line organizations did not use the two-way symmetric model all the time. Excellent organizations know what it takes to function in society, both for the short term and for the long term. They know that the two-way symmetric model provides a framework for ethical communicational practices, and they are wedded to the model.

Even excellent organizations, however, engage in what has been known as the "mixed-motive game" (Murphy, 1991, p. 115). In mixed-motive games, parties on both sides of an issue pursue their own interests, but both also realize that the outcome must be satisfactory to both parties.

Putting the model into practice for schools, it might work as follows (Dozier, 1995):

> In thinking of symmetrical and asymmetrical practices as parts of a common mixed-motive game, knowledge of both models makes sense. As organizations pursue their own interests in relations with publics, [principals] try—from time to time—to persuade publics that their organizations are right on an issue. At times [principals] try to convince publics to behave as their

organizations want. Sometimes, [principals] try to manipulate publics scientifically. Indeed, publics will likewise follow similar asymmetrical strategies to persuade, convince, and manipulate organizations. However, organizations and publics also need to find equilibrium, a middle position, between the desired outcomes of each. Such equilibrium must be sufficiently satisfactory so that neither the publics nor organizations have cause to regret their actions, given how the other side would have responded. Publics and organizations can be described as cooperative antagonists, looking for a compromise around an issue in which true differences exist between the parties. (pp. 47–48)

The issue for principals, then, is the following: Should they attempt to persuade their stakeholders to concur with the district's beliefs? That would be the historical way of doing business. Or is the principal's central mission to be responsive to the public's interests? That would certainly be in line with the new leadership training principals have received. When there is an obvious conflict between these two positions, what is the principal to do? Well, that is when principals employ their communication management skills and use the mixed-motive approach. They can take comfort knowing that nearly all the best managed organizations in the world use it occasionally.

Principals considering the mixed-motive approach need to be clear about one issue, however. Principals who normally practice one-way, top-down communication with their publics should not switch to the mixed-motive approach. That will not work. Principals have to build up a reserve of trust and respect with their Partners through regular two-way symmetric communication before ever deciding to occasionally employ the mixed-motive approach. Then it might work. Principals know that occasionally they are going to have to use one of the asymmetric models (e.g., when a school district attempts to manipulate the public to endorse the school district's position). If they are shrewd, they will gently alert their closest Partners to this bureaucratic fact of life before it becomes a reality, and they can address it as a partnership when it becomes necessary.

Principals need to be confident of their relationships with their key stakeholders. Principals need to understand that their first priority is to ensure they maintain the two-way symmetric model of communication with their Partners. If the relationship with them is strong and built on trust and respect, then the Partners may tolerate the principal using the seemingly contradictory philosophies of symmetric and asymmetric approaches occasionally.

Partners Can Also Play the Game

Of course, principals need to understand—and tolerate—Partners doing the same thing. As Figure 3.2 depicts, however, both Partners can engage in the mixed-motive approach, playing for their own gains. The "game," however, works only if both parties remember that underlying this contest is a recollection that it is in their mutual best interest to ensure that it is played out to the end with a mutual "win-win" scenario, or the underlying symmetric philosophy is in jeopardy.

It is important for principals to be grounded in the belief that the two-way symmetric approach is as much a philosophy as it is a method. Of course, occasionally, principals will engage in the mixed-motive approach. Principals must understand, however, that what they are engaged in is "a sliding scale of cooperation and competition in which organizational needs must of necessity be balanced against constituents' needs, but never lose their primacy" (Murphy, 1991, p. 27). In other words, the needs of the Partners are important, but principals can never forget that they are employed by the district and work for the superintendent and the school board.

On the other hand, the principal's tactical use of asymmetric models cannot jeopardize the larger cooperative framework. All communication tactics, from all players, must operate within the framework

Figure 3.2   The principal and the partners can engage occasionally in mixed-motive communication practices as long as they remember that both sides win only if they commit to the two-way symmetric communication model.

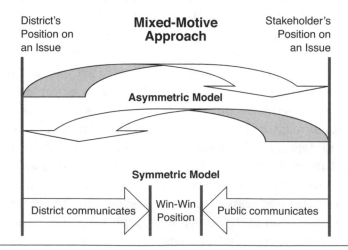

suggestive of symmetric practices that include the following (Dozier, 1995, 1997):

- Parties have no malevolent intent.
- Each party would like to be truthful.
- Parties would like to reach a compromise.
- Parties expect power to be used gracefully.
- Parties expect both sides to abide by the law.
- Parties expect that all joint agreements will be honored.

The two-way symmetric approach is like a badge of honor that principals wear. It signifies their identity as a school leader. It says that when a problem or issue arises, they are prepared to talk about it honestly and openly with their key stakeholders, to seek their input in solving the matter, and to share the resolution of it with them. It says that those who make up their partnership are involved in the decision making of their schools. It says that the principals are an advocate for the students, the parents, the faculty and staff, the community, and their school. That is the principals' basic grounding. Thus, the basic communication model followed by the principal is the two-way symmetric model. Occasionally, however, with great care, the principal may use a mixed-motive approach to address an issue or problem.

Principals will probably be most comfortable trying to use a straight symmetry model as much as possible for the simple reason that it tends to be consistent with all the other characteristics of the school improvement efforts under way at the school. Alas, the journey seldom ever goes as planned.

For example, imagine a secondary school principal who has just left a personnel hearing involving a football coach. The coach has been accused of an infraction in his coaching role. He has admitted it, and both he and the union representative sitting with him through the hearing agree that the school has the right to dismiss him as head coach. The principal asks the coach to resign instead. The coach does, and all parties agree that they will issue a statement announcing the coach's resignation with no mention of the infraction or any admission of wrongdoing on his part.

Nothing, of course, is ever that simple. Let's say that in this case the starting quarterback has publicly threatened to transfer to a private school in the community if the coach quits or is fired, and that his father, a prominent school booster, is prepared to "go to the media and the school board" if necessary. The coach has many Friends on the faculty, and they too say they would be upset if he "got a raw deal."

Obviously, this is not a matter that the principal can discuss in his usual settings with all hands assembled. It is a personnel issue, and the settlement required all parties to remain quiet about the incident. In this case, the principal would be well advised to write a formal memo that spells out the terms of the settlement in as little detail as possible. The statement should mention plans to name a replacement soon. It may cite the outgoing coach's previous record of accomplishment, but it should not contain comments about regrets over his resignation, which would be dishonest.

The memo should be reviewed by the coach and the union representative and then distributed through formal channels as the only official release. It is an old "public information" method, but one that is best used in this situation. At that point, all parties involved should be reminded that it is in nobody's best interest to comment further on the dismissal.

Occasionally, principals are going to find themselves caught between the school board and the employee unions in wage and salary tussles. The principals are district managers and as such know they must exhibit management solidarity. Some staff may challenge principals in this case. They may wonder how principals can be "partners" with regard to addressing common interests in the school but have different interests with regard to something as basic as their Partners' salaries and working conditions.

Principals may well have to resort to using one-way communication to the union employees regarding personnel matters until the labor issues are settled. Principals should remember that they should "go formal" only when necessary but otherwise retain their symmetric communication habits on other issues involving the Partners. It is important that Partners recognize that labor disputes do get resolved, and the important work of the school continues.

How the Central Office Views the Principal

Effective principals are advocates for their schools, and this will not go unnoticed by the central office. It is an admirable trait, and principals will be applauded for their leadership on behalf of their Partners—up to a point.

Principals who practice the two-way symmetric model of communication with their partnerships are a force to be reckoned with because everybody in the central office will know the principals have very good relationships with their staffs, parents, and communities.

In other words, these schools have a lot going for them, and they can shake up the system if they want.

Note that principals with strong school partnerships probably have already rattled central office administrators. To some extent, a partnership with its resulting action team and annual plan (see Chapter 4) may have inadvertently marginalized some central office administrators. Partnerships may be less likely to call on central office specialists or, when they do, be much more aggressive in laying out what they want rather than simply taking what is offered. At the very least, the nature of the relationship between the school and the central office is in flux when the principal has a two-way symmetric model of communication in place and empowers a partnership to create a family-like school.

In some school districts, the changed relationship between the empowered school and the central office will be deemed by both parties to be a success story and paraded before other schools as an example of how they too could be operating. In other districts, however, central office staff may resent a partnership with its action team and yearly plan and 3-year goals. What, after all, does that say about the role of central office administrators and their importance? Although savvy principals will do their best to make the Enablers part of the school's partnership, it behooves the school leaders to cover their backs when dealing with central office administrators who may not yet have learned that "management" is out and "leadership" is in.

Communication Skills Empower the Principal

Principals with the skills to manage communication within and among the stakeholders of a school soon learn that they can use these same skills for other purposes. For example, principals who have mastered both symmetric and asymmetric skills internally may be tempted to use them to gain the school an advantage in the public area.

A principal of a high school in a city with four public high schools may resent the fact that resources are tight and her school board is determined to treat each high school "fairly" with regard to next year's tight budget. Her key publics believe her school needs many more resources to accomplish its goals. It clearly is not going to be able to do so with the allocation she expects from the school board, however.

The principal could meet with her partnership and strategize about what they could do to publicize her situation to the board. Plans could be made to stage a special science fair at the high school that would highlight the superiority of her faculty and the shortage of their lab equipment. A story could be planted in the local newspaper about how the entire coaching staff of the boys and girls basketball teams is considering resigning because of the deplorable condition of the gymnasium. A fundraising campaign could be mounted immediately, cochaired by the sports editor of the paper, with an editorial noting how absurd it is that taxpayers had to raise money for a public school over and above what the district allocated. All these and other ideas could be floated without the principal's initials ever appearing on a memo.

Principals will find themselves caught up in the dilemma of putting the interests of their schools above the interests of the district at large. This is an ongoing issue in districts in which some schools serve much more affluent student populations and tend to find it easier to create and energize powerful school, family, and community partnerships than do schools serving lower-income students. Should the spoils go to those best able to manipulate the system? Principals and their Partners will ask themselves these questions and struggle with the answers, of course. An effective principal will have the communication management skills to take whatever course of action they decide; at the same time, one with integrity will also do what is best for the students and the community.

Of course, a principal can go too far and cut himself off entirely from the district office. One of the disadvantages of "symmetry" is that it "tends to discourage innovation and encourage custom and tradition" (Murphy, 1991, p. 124). In other words, the principal and his stakeholders can get too close, and together they isolate themselves from the district and its larger vision for what is needed for the entire community. This enviably leads to a change in the school's leadership.

Summary

In this chapter, four types of public relations models were introduced: (a) press agentry/publicity, (b) public information, (c) two-way asymmetric, and (d) two-way symmetric. The public information model is the most popular and certainly the most commonly used by schools.

An international survey of organizations identified the characteristics of companies that tended to rely on the asymmetric models versus those companies that used the symmetric model. It found that the companies that used the two-way symmetric model had much in common with public schools today that are transparent, focused on school reform, open to free exchange of information within, innovative, open to new ideas, practice decentralized management, and attempt to resolve conflict through negotiation and compromise.

Picking up on this finding, principals were urged to adopt a philosophy that supports the symmetric model and practice it as the communication management method whenever possible. Even the most successful organizations in the survey, however, tended to use a mixed-motive approach when managing their communication. This enabled them to operate with a corporate philosophy that supported the symmetric approach but allowed for the occasional use of the asymmetric models. Therefore, school principals were advised that they need to master communication management strategies because although they will attempt to operate schools using symmetric models of communication, occasionally they will have to use asymmetric models. Their skill in doing this while maintaining the loyalty of their stakeholders will be a major factor in their ability to accomplish their goals.

4

Strengthening School-Family-Community Partnerships

The first three chapters of this book established a few assumptions that are worth reviewing here:

- Effective principals are going to establish a school, family, and community partnership.
- With such a partnership in place, the old-fashioned communication models previously used to communicate with stakeholders (i.e., primarily the top-down, "public information" model) are not going to accomplish the objectives of the partnership.
- Principals are going to want to implement the two-way symmetric model of communication for use with all the stakeholders that constitute their partnership whenever they can.
- To manage the communications process effectively, principals are going to have to know when and how "publics" are created among their likely Partners, and what their issues or problems are, so that communication strategies to address these emerging publics can be devised and implemented.

The authors' understanding of school, family, and community partnerships derives from 30 years of friendship and collaboration with Joyce L. Epstein, a principal research scientist at the Center for Social Organization of Schools at Johns Hopkins University. Although other scholars do work in this field, few have gained the scholarly reputation or earned the respect of school practitioners to rival this nationally known researcher.

Epstein has written more than 100 publications on the organization and effects of school, classroom, family, and peer environments, with many of them focused on school, family, and community connections. In 1995, she established the National Network of Partnership Schools to highlight the impact of her recommended practices for school improvement. This chapter borrows heavily from her work.[1]

Understanding the Theory for Elementary Schools

When elementary schools operated as bureaucracies, administrators tended to view families as separate from the school and children as students. Then researchers who study social organizations came up with a different way of viewing the basic components of school, family, and communities. They tried organizing them differently. The results from what they learned were amazing. If educators view students as children rather than as students, they are likely to view both the family and the community as partners with the school.

When the elementary school views parents and the community as partners, the resulting partnership can improve school programs and school climate, provide family services and support, increase parents' skills and leadership, connect families with others in the school and the community, and help teachers with their work.

Above all, the resulting partnerships can help children succeed in school and in later life because principals begin to view students as children. They begin to realize that when they, teachers, parents, students, and others view one another as partners in education, a caring community forms.

The first step has been taken. The principals are now calling their students "children." Now the second challenge is at hand. It is called getting out of the "rhetoric rut." That is where many educators get stuck: They say they want to do something but, not knowing how to proceed, stay right where they are.

The second step is to assemble the teachers and find out if they do not agree that almost all the families involved with the school care about their children and want them to succeed. Most of these parents or other caregivers will be eager to obtain better information from the school so they can be better partners in their children's education. So far, so good.

Now principals need some kind of involvement to get started building partnerships. Epstein suggested six major types that have been studied for years. They have been introduced into elementary, middle, and secondary schools throughout the country; studied; documented; and written up for others to review (Epstein, 1992; Epstein & Connors, 1995: Epstein & Sanders, 2000).

Each type of involvement includes many different practices. Each type also presents particular challenges that must be met to involve all families. Then too, each type is likely to lead to different results for students, parents, teaching practices, and school climates. Consequently, it is not easy for the partnership to make choices about which practices to use. Problems will occur with each one. They must be resolved if all the families are going to be reached and involved in the best way possible. Of course, as each problem is resolved, the resolution will in turn create its own set of problems. And on and on it goes.

In her handbook, Epstein (2002a) lists sample practices for each of the six types of involvement (Table 4.1). The sample practices Epstein and colleagues list for "communicating" are as follows (Epstein, 2002a, p. 14):

Conferences with every parent at least once a year, with follow-ups as needed;

Language translators assist families, as needed;

Weekly or monthly folders of student work sent home for review and comments;

Parent-student pickup of report cards, with conferences on improving grades;

Regular schedule of useful notices, memos, phone calls, newsletters, and other communication;

Clear information on choosing schools or courses, programs, and activities within schools; and

Clear information on all school policies, programs, reforms, and transitions.

Table 4.1 Framework of Six Types of Involvement for Comprehensive Programs of Partnerships for Elementary Schools

Parenting	Communicating	Volunteering	Learning at Home	Decision Making	Collaborating With the Community
Help all families establish home environments to support children as students.	Design effective forms of school-to-home and home-to-school communication about school programs and their children's progress.	Recruit and organize parent help and support.	Provide information and ideas to families about how to help students at home with homework and other curriculum-related activities, decisions, and planning.	Include parents in school decisions, developing parent leaders and representatives.	Identify and integrate resources and services from the community to strengthen school programs, family practices, and student learning and development.

SOURCE: Epstein (2002a, p. 14).

The communication activities promoted by Epstein are very similar to the two-way symmetric model practiced by the best companies in the Grunig survey and advocated by leading communication management experts. That is, the educators are as interested in listening to the parents talk about the children as they are in having the parents listen to them talk about their children. The communication is two-way, with the intent by both parties to reach mutual understanding and resolve any disputes. That does not mean the school does not occasionally use the public information model when it has basic information it wishes to pass on about upcoming meetings or information about school-related news. Also, the principal may occasionally resort to a few press agentry gimmicks to get the families involved in a back-to-school events. Overall, however, the communication climate is characterized as open, two-way, and symmetric.

As soon as the partners establish any type of partnership activity, they need to examine it to determine what particular challenges it presents to families who wish to participate. Epstein and colleagues provide the following checklist (Epstein 2002a, p. 15):

- Review the readability, clarity, form, and frequency of all memos, notices, and other print and nonprint communication.
- Consider parents who do not speak English well, do not read well, or need large type.
- Review the quality of major communication (e.g., the schedule, content, and structure of conferences, newsletters, report cards, and others).
- Establish clear two-way channels for communication from home to school and from school to home.

Experience has taught Epstein much over the years. Regarding communication in partnership programs, it is not simply two-way; "it's three-way and many-ways" (Epstein, 2002a, p. 15) when it comes to connecting schools, families, students, and the community.

If a school leader is thinking that creating partnerships sounds like a lot of work, Epstein would agree with him and say "don't try it on your own." A principal can be the leader in getting the ball rolling, but it will require a team—she calls it an "action team for partnerships"—to create the proper structure (Epstein, 2002a, p. 18). By whatever name, the team oversees the development of the involvement efforts and the integration of all family and community connections into a single, unified plan and program.

Regarding family, involvement is clearly meant to mean more than just mothers. Children do better in school when their fathers are involved, even if their fathers do not live with them. Shedlin (2004) notes,

> Research shows that both in two-parent and single-parent families, the involvement of fathers exerts a distinct influence on whether children repeat a grade, get mostly "A's," enjoy school, and participate in extracurricular activities—even after controlling for mothers' involvement in school. (p. 24)

Grandparents and siblings can also be important participants in a child's life.

Epstein (2002a) suggests five critical steps that schools should take to develop their capacity to sustain strong school, family, and community connections.

Step 1. Create an Action Team

The team should include at least three teachers from different grade levels; three parents with children in different grade levels; one administrator; one member from the community at large; and, at the high school level, at least two students from different grade levels. The team may also include a cafeteria worker, a social worker, a counselor, or a school psychologist. The leader may be any member of the team as long as the leader has the respect of the other members and has good communication skills. In addition to group planning, members serve as the chair or cochair of one of six subcommittees for each type of involvement.

Step 2. Obtain Funds and Other Support

The team needs a modest budget to support staff development, to pay for lead teachers at each school to serve as action team for partnership chairs, to set up demonstration programs, and for other partnership expenses. The team must also be given sufficient time and social support to do its work.

Step 3: Identify Starting Points

The team starts by collecting information about the school's current practices of partnership. Then the team determines current strengths and needed changes in these ongoing efforts. The team determines what teachers expect of families and what families expect of teachers and other school personnel. The team determines which families are difficult to reach and what can be done to communicate with and engage these families in their children's education. Finally, the team asks, How might family and community connections assist the school in helping more students reach higher goals and achieve greater success?

Step 4: Develop a 3-Year Outline and a 1-Year Action Plan

The team decides where it wants to be in 3 years. Then it produces a detailed 1-year action plan that includes the specific activities that will be implemented, improved, or maintained for each type of involvement; a timeline of monthly actions needed for each activity; identification of the subcommittee chair who will be responsible either for each type of involvement or for involvement to promote specific goals for student success; identification of the teachers, parents, students, or others who will assist with the implementation of each activity; indicators of how the implementation and results of each majority activity will be assessed; and other details of importance to the action team.

Step 5: Continue Planning and Working

The action team should schedule an annual presentation and celebration of progress at the school so that all participants know about the work that has been done each year. Each year, the team updates the outline and develops a detailed 1-year action plan for the following year.

With the benefit of her experience, Epstein and colleagues note that the development of a partnership program is a process, not a single event. Principals should not expect every teacher, family member, student, or community group to engage in all activities across all types of involvement at once. Nor should principals assume every activity will succeed with all families. Over time, however, with good planning, thoughtful implementation, well-designed activities, and good communication management, increasingly more families and teachers will learn to work with one another on behalf of the children whose interests they share. The first step is for the principal to decide to make the partnership a priority.

Connecting Partnerships and Publics

It may help to revisit what the reader already knows about "good communication management" in the context of the reader's new-found enthusiasm for school-family-community partnerships and determine how it can be applied.

First, the reader will clearly recognize that any elementary principal who engages in a school-family-community partnership is practicing the two-way symmetric model of communication. The exclusive use of one-way asymmetric models by the principal would be frowned on in the trusting and respecting atmosphere built up among the stakeholders in an active partnership.

Second, the stakeholders involved in an active partnership are by definition an active public. That is, it is a group of individuals that recognizes a common issue, communicates among itself about it, seeks outside information about it, and then organizes to do something about it. This is exactly the kind of active public that principals want in schools of excellence.

Third, the partnership spends a great deal of time and effort engaging in various communication efforts to increase "latent" and "aware" audiences' awareness of and involvement in the partnership.

What communication research says, and research in schools says, is that one effective way of increasing people's receptivity to messages is to increase their involvement. In other words, Epstein realizes that parents, faculty, and students who are more involved in partnerships are more likely to communicate with one another about it. Communication researchers know that if people feel involvement with an issue, they are more likely to read and retain what they read about it.

Thus, if a principal wants to increase the likelihood that messages she sends home with the children will be read by the parents, she should increase the parents' involvement with the school. The more involved they are with the school, the greater the likelihood they are to read messages their children bring home from the school.

Relatedly, if the parents buy into the notion of the partnership and understand what it is trying to accomplish, then they will be much more likely to read messages that their children bring home. Again, communication researchers have demonstrated that "problem recognition" increases processing and information-seeking behavior. If the parents believe they are involved, they are much more apt to engage in communication with the school. They also are more likely to be active participants in the partnership.

The same is also true for community partners who interact with the schools. The first step is for the schools to make the partners feel involved, which probably means first learning what they bring to the table rather than simply expecting them to fill a role that the school has prescribed. Whereas local businesses and industry may be more than willing to simply write checks or serve as corporate sponsors, other groups, such as national service or volunteer organizations such as the Boy Scouts and neighborhood boys' clubs, may be offended if asked for such donations. The latter may be better collaborators around student-centered activities. Knowing the difference in the kinds of partners to create among the community groups and how to approach each of them is key in any communication strategy. The following are examples of community partners (Sanders, 2002, p. 32):

Businesses/corporations

Universities and educational institutions

Health care organizations

Government and military agencies

National service and volunteer organizations

Faith-based organizations

Senior citizen organizations

Cultural and recreational institutions

Other community organizations

Community individuals

For example, principals might well approach a business or corporation if they need someone to sponsor a school festival. They would not approach a faith-based organization or recreational institution for that purpose, however. Principals might approach a community organization or a service organization to sponsor a scholarship for a student, though, and involve senior citizen organizations when in search of tutors. Universities are not likely to write many checks, but they frequently house research centers or even research projects that may have overlap with the school's partnership's interests. At the very least, they have graduate students in need of dissertation topics who may be willing to help with the action team's evaluation efforts.

The communication from the school to each of these potential partners should be designed to make them aware of the formation of the partnership and their unique role in it. Principals should play to the importance of their involvement. They should be reminded of what they have to contribute and how it will make a difference with regard to what the school and the parents are trying to accomplish.

The first communication should be designed to get the potential partner to invite the school to sit down and discuss the partnership face to face. That meeting should be designed to get a commitment to some level of involvement, even if it is modest at first. Communication with the partner from then on should be designed to move the aware partner to an active partner over time.

Focusing on Middle and Secondary Schools

Although research suggests that partnerships among families, communities, and schools remain important for students' success even as they grow older, studies on partnerships reveal that family involvement tends to decrease as children pass from the elementary grades into middle and senior high schools (Simon, 2002, p. 235). Perhaps for that reason, few secondary schools have implemented comprehensive partnership programs (Epstein, 2002b, p. 220). Consequently, this book devotes less attention to the topic of partnerships for middle and secondary schools than it does for elementary schools simply because there is much less to talk about when focusing on the higher grades.

Of course, the emphasis could change because secondary schools are starting to become the targets of reform throughout the country. In 2005, for example, the U.S. Department of Education announced a major initiative to hold high schools accountable for student achievement. Also, the Gates Foundation said it was going to significantly increase spending on its already major effort to reduce the size of high schools in hopes that they would become more "user friendly." In addition, a group of states said they intended to work together to develop ways to make the high school years more meaningful for students. Although some scholars have expressed healthy skepticism about these efforts to reform secondary education given the many expectations society had for it (Ravitch, 2005, p. 25), it is possible that the attention will spur parental interest in school partnerships. That alone is reason enough to at least explore them here.

One of the first tasks for any middle or secondary principal, of course, is to get the families of their students comfortable with their teachers. Most are uncertain about how to relate to their students' teachers. The families lack information about the middle and high school curriculum, policies, and requirements for college admissions. Families tend to live farther away from their students' schools than they did when they attended elementary schools; consequently, families are less likely to get involved as their children get older. Of course, as their children get older, they want more independence and arc less likely to encourage their families' involvement in their schooling.

Creating Partnerships Is a Lot of Work

The need for partnerships at the high school is evident, but creating an environment in which they flourish is more complicated for the middle and secondary principal than it is for the typical elementary school principal. In short, creating partnerships at middle and secondary schools is difficult in any case, especially for their principals. Fortunately, evidence suggests the investment that goes into middle and secondary school partnerships pays great dividends.

Analyses based on reports from the parents of more than 11,000 high school students and from more than 1,000 high school principals in the National Education Longitudinal Study of 1988 enabled Johns Hopkins University researchers to conclude the following about the effects of partnerships on student success and the relationship between school outreach and family involvement (Table 4.2):

> Schools, families, and communities continue to partner in a range of ways through teenagers' last year of high school.

> Regardless of teenagers' achievement or background, high school and family partnerships have a positive influence on teenagers' grades, course credits completed, attendance, behavior, and school preparedness.

> Regardless of family background or school context, when high schools reach out to involve families, families respond with increased involvement.

Thus, although school-family-community partnerships at the middle and high school are difficult to implement and are fairly rare, the case can be made that they are definitely worthwhile.

Epstein and colleagues (2002) devote a fair portion of their helpful handbook to middle and secondary schools. As they do for their elementary principals, Epstein and coauthors outline what middle and secondary principals need to do to establish partnerships in their schools. As with elementary schools, middle and secondary schools should use a framework of six types of family and community involvement to

Table 4.2   The Influence of High School Outreach on Family

When High Schools . . .	Parents Were More Likely to . . .
Contacted parents about teens' plans after high school	Attend college and career-planning workshops and talk with teens about college and careers
Contacted parents about volunteering	Volunteer as an audience member at school activities
Gave parents information about how to help teens study	Work with their teens on homework
Contacted parents about school-related issues	Talk with teens about school-related issues
Formally recruited and trained parent volunteers	Volunteer for the school
Encourage parent-school associations	Join the PTA/PTO and attend meetings

SOURCE: Simon (2002, p. 243).

guide their partnerships. The handbook discusses sample practices for each type of involvement as well as some of the challenges that all schools must face if they hope to achieve successful partnerships. The handbook also provides examples of results that middle and secondary schools can logically expect to achieve from each type of involvement for students, families, and educators (Table 4.3).

What principals know from their study of communication theory is that families who feel more involved with their children's school are also more likely to process information and to seek out information about the school. Consequently, principals who wish to increase family involvement in parenting, learning at home, and decision-making activities should concentrate initially on getting the parents hooked on volunteering.

Schools can use family members to serve as boosters or supporters of extracurricular clubs or organize and improve activities, such as school stores and fairs. They can be homeroom parents and sports or club contacts; operate telephone trees; run "welcome wagons" for new families; or work as mentors, coaches, tutors, and leaders of afterschool programs.

The challenge, of course, is for principals to ensure that volunteers feel appreciated. Also, the term should be broadly defined so

Table 4.3   Framework of Six Types of Involvement for Comprehensive Programs of Partnerships for Middle and Secondary Schools

Parenting	Communicating	Volunteering	Learning at Home	Decision Making	Collaborating With the Community
Help all families strengthen parenting skills, understand adolescent development, and set home conditions to support learning at every grade level.	Increase school-to-home and home-to-school communication about school programs and student progress through notices, memos, conferences, report cards, newsletters, phone, e-mail, and Internet messages.	Improve recruitment, training, and schedules to involve parents and others as volunteers and as audiences at the school or in other locations to support students and school programs.	Involve families with their children in academic learning activities at home that are coordinated with students' class work and that contribute to student success in school.	Include families in developing mission statements and in designing, reviewing, and improving school policies that affect their children and families.	Draw upon and coordinate the resources of community businesses, cultural, civic, and religious organizations, senior citizen groups, and so on to strengthen school programs, family practices, and student learning.

SOURCE: Epstein (2002b, pp. 221–227).

that parents and family members who come to school as audiences for school plays and sporting events, assemblies, and other activities that support student work are recognized as volunteers. The hours during which volunteers are welcome need to be flexible to take advantage of the different working arrangements of the families involved. A coordinator may be necessary to ensure that volunteers are recruited widely and used wisely.

Along with the volunteering activity is the communicating activity. This consists of a heavy dose of two-way communication between the school and the families involving all kinds of notes, memos, newsletters, phone calls, and face-to-face meetings.

The basic idea is to give families the information they need about their middle school and high school children's progress and problems. Families need to understand the criteria, for example, that teachers use to complete report cards. Families need to know how to interpret interim progress reports. Conferences among families, students, teachers, and possibly counselors may be necessary to ensure that students take responsibility for learning.

Other communication from the school to the families contains basic information about calendars of upcoming events, student work, and parent questions and responses. Increasingly, middle and high schools are providing families with the e-mail addresses and voice-mail numbers of their children's teachers and counselors to encourage ongoing two-way communication.

A major challenge, of course, confronts every principal who has significant numbers of students whose families do not speak English at home. Extra effort must be made to ensure—to the extent possible—that materials sent home are written in the native language of the families receiving them. Also, principals need to ensure that interpreters are on hand when these families come to school for conferences with their children's teachers.

Just as the elementary principals do, the middle and secondary principals need to follow the advice outlined in Epstein et al.'s (2002) handbook and create their own action teams for partnerships consisting of teachers, parents, administrators, and others. These teams write the school's annual action plan for the partnership. The plan describes the activities, how they will be implemented and funded, and how they will be evaluated. Savvy principals will join the National Network of Partnership Schools at Johns Hopkins to obtain ongoing professional development for their partnerships (www.partner shipschools.org).

Summary

Effective school principals are either already in school-parent-community partnerships or are seriously considering establishing one. Certainly principals operating transparent schools with open communication between themselves and their key stakeholders— using two-way symmetric communication—are practically functioning in a partnership relationship anyway. So it is time to formalize it. There is no better way than to get acquainted with the methods suggested by Epstein and colleagues from the Center for Social Organization of Schools at Johns Hopkins University.

This chapter introduced Epstein's six types of involvement: parenting, communicating, volunteering, learning at home, decision making, and collaborating with the community. It detailed what she has to say about how the communicating practices work and the kinds of challenges they present. It then suggested how principals' knowledge of publics would facilitate their working with partnerships and improve the likelihood of success in their communication efforts.

The chapter concluded by stating that Epstein and colleagues have written a handbook for getting partnerships started that have a high likelihood of success in elementary, middle, and secondary schools. In addition, her research center maintains a Web site that links together a national network of partnerships that provides ongoing technical support for new and old members alike. Principals searching for an edge would be wise to give both the handbook and the Web site some study.

Note

1. Readers interested in establishing a school-family-community partnership may want to read Epstein et al.'s (2002) book. Readers who want to learn about the literature that underlies the field may want to read her other major work, *School, Family, and Community Partnerships: Preparing Educators and Improving Schools* (2001).

PART II

The Strategic Management of Communication

Part II moves away from theory and is much more concerned about practical applications of communication. Chapter 5, for example, consists of three case studies. Three principals in three different kinds of schools in three very different areas of the country use communication management skills to provide leadership to address challenges they face. School leaders fresh from the theory chapters should find the practical applications of this knowledge interesting reading.

Part II also introduces the reader to the fact that although school leaders are trained to think of themselves as the initiators of messages, often they are apt to be on the receiving end of the messages as well. Simply put, they are cornered in their office by irate or frustrated parents or community members who demand to know why things are the way they are and why they cannot be changed and changed immediately. Other times, of course, the principal is the communicator but with little time to prepare a message, such as when a crisis hits. Every school has a crisis management plan in place, and the school leader knows how to implement it. That is not the problem. The principal will see to the children's safety, first and foremost. Afterwards, however, when the assessment is done and people are asking what could have been done better, they are going to point the finger at the principal and say, "He should have done a better job of communicating with us about what was going on."

Amazingly, that is often exactly what happens after a crisis: The principal is blamed for not having kept everybody informed during the crisis about what was taking place. Sure, he was busy. Yes, he did his job. And okay, he followed procedure, but he should have notified the parents, kept the teachers better informed, at least called the PTA president, or stayed in better contact with the central office.

They are correct. Today, in an era when practically every adult has a cell phone and every office a computer, it seems that everyone expects either a call or an e-mail if something unusual occurs at a school during school hours. By now, principals should realize that any event at their schools is going to be picked up and reported to the outside world immediately anyway. So their publics are going to hear about the crisis initially from someone; when they come searching for information, they expect their principals to be able to supply it. Woe be those who fail this test (see the case studies in Chapter 6).

Chapters 9 and 10 present practical suggestions for how a principal can be savvy about communicating with stakeholders.

5

Applying Communication Management in Different Settings

The best way to learn communication management is from a seasoned principal, and this chapter introduces three of the best in the business. One is an elementary school principal from Corpus Christi, Texas; the other is a secondary school principal from Fargo, North Dakota; and the third is a middle school principal from a suburban community in northern Virginia, near Washington, D.C. Each of them, in their own story, demonstrates an insight of their particular stakeholders and a skillful use of communication management. In one story, however, a focus on one set of critical stakeholders threatens to jeopardize a relationship with another. In the second story, it becomes obvious that even the best of plans seem to come unraveled when a crisis hits. Finally, the third story demonstrates just how much work is associated with communication management if it is to pay off year in and year out.

Three lessons emerge from these stories to guide principals. First, effective communication management begins with the active, ongoing involvement of the principal. The principal is the school leader, and the stakeholders clearly expect the principal to be the primary communicator. Second, having said that, the principal cannot do it alone. Although communication management is the principal's ongoing responsibility, she needs to enlist the school's stakeholders in the process too. A transparent school with shared decision making requires the involvement of all partners in the communication process. Such a process cannot depend on a top-down flow of information to function. Also, during a crisis, even when the stakeholders expect the principal to provide leadership, too many stakeholders need to be informed immediately for the principal to do it alone. Third, a principal who uses effective communication management tools will reap tremendous benefits. The principal will capture the support of stakeholders and hold their trust and respect when they are needed most.

Principals know that when a problem occurs, they need to alert key publics about it immediately. During the school year, principals are faced with many challenges or problems that require them to notify many of their partners immediately with a "heads-up" notice or alert. Few of these problems get the blood stirring quite like news of a student on campus with a gun. A school safety issue is a hot-button topic for every stakeholder group, and for most partners—parents, faculty, neighbors, staff, volunteers, media, the police department, the fire department, the central office, the school board, friends, peers, and the students—it is of paramount importance. They want the principal to communicate fully and accurately what is transpiring in the school regarding the incident as soon as the principal learns about it; there are no excuses for delaying or withholding the information.

Most principals will go through their entire careers and never have to deal with a school violence situation. They all should be prepared to do so, however. If they are, they will be prepared to handle nearly any communication management crisis that occurs. And for sure, a crisis of one kind or other will occur regularly.

Communication Management Requires Good Planning and Execution

Consider, for example, the story of Richard Warner. In the fall of 2003, Warner had been the principal at Fargo South High School in Fargo, North Dakota, for 25 years. He was a popular principal, well liked by the school's stakeholders. He ran a transparent school in which problems were openly discussed among his stakeholders. He was accessible to people and they knew it; likewise, he believed he could call on Fargo South supporters from throughout the community to rally around the school when needed. Clearly, he practiced a two-way symmetric model of communication management.

At 11 a.m. on a chilly October morning, however, his communication management techniques were put to the test. It began when a study hall teacher slipped a note into the principal's office saying a student in her class had a weapon in his possession. Warner was in a meeting, but his assistant principal (now principal), Todd Bertsch, and a "resource officer" (one of five armed Fargo Police officers assigned to the secondary schools in the city) went to the classroom and removed the student and his possessions from the classroom.

When Assistant Principal Bertsch and the officer had the student in the principal's office, they asked him if he had a weapon. He said he did and produced a pellet gun. Although relatively harmless compared to a regular firearm, it was designed to resemble a Glock 9 mm; "and believe me, it did," said Warner.

Student Struck in the Leg

The study hall teacher said that she had been alerted to the student and the weapon by another student. That individual, when questioned by school officials, said that the student who had the gun had fired it at him prior to class and had struck him in the leg. "The gun shoots either BBs or plastic shot," said Warner. "In this case, it was loaded with plastic shot. The student who had been shot wasn't hurt. He didn't even have a welt or a sting."

Meanwhile, the student with the gun admitted to shooting his classmate as well as to firing another shot into a nearby wastebasket. At that point, procedure dictated the process. Warner was called out of his meeting. The superintendent was notified. The police, of course, were already on the scene. The boy's parents were called, and his father was asked to come to the school. He was informed that his son was being suspended for 10 days pending further investigation. The boy was then released into the custody of his parents.

By noon, Warner and his staff began to hear reports that other students may have been shot by the student during morning classes, so the afternoon was spent tracking down these students and taking their statements. Before school let out, Warner said six more students confirmed they had been shot by the student with the pellet gun inside the school.

Warner and Bertsch immediately called the parents of each of these six students. They wanted the parents to hear from them that their children had been shot by a pellet gun while at school that morning and that they were okay and the student who had done the shooting had been caught.

Parents Appreciated Calls

The calls worked as Warner had hoped. Because of years spent building good relationships and trust, all six groups of parents said they appreciated the calls and agreed that they saw no reason for their children to be dismissed early from school if they did not request it. In fact, several of the parents called Warner back and pleaded on behalf of the student who shot the gun. They hoped he would not expel the student because they believed he needed help; they did not think expelling him was the correct solution.

The day finally came to an end, and Warner and his administrative staff congratulated themselves on a job well done. The student with the gun had been caught and removed without incident. No students had been injured. The school day had not been badly disrupted. The parents involved had all been contacted and were understanding. The central office was satisfied with the way events were handled. The police were on top of the paperwork, which would take 2 or 3 days to finish. That meant media coverage, if any, would not occur until later. For all practical purposes, it appeared that the loose ends were almost wrapped up. Of course, that was not to be the case.

Warner had not said anything about the incident to the faculty, the primary group among his Partner stakeholders. They were furious. Several teachers heard about the incident from parents of their students that evening at the supermarket or at afterschool activities. By the time Warner sent an explanation to the faculty, 48 hours after the fact, it was at least 40 hours too late.

Warner also did not send a note to the critical members of his partnership stakeholder group: parent volunteers and committee members, PTA officers, partnering community groups, and key corporate partners. He believed that the media eventually would fill them in on the story. It took 4 days for the media to report the story, and by then the story had spread through the community by word of mouth.

The principal's official version of what happened that morning, had he posted it on the school's Web site, might have damped some of the rumors and discredited some of the wilder versions of the stories making the rounds during those 4 days. Warner said the PTA officials, with whom he is particularly close, said he did not suffer much from that oversight. They agreed, however, that it probably would have been a good idea if they had heard the official version of the story from him first.

The lesson from Warner's experience is that all principals need to have a comprehensive communication plan that outlines specific steps and responsibilities for everyone on the communication team in place before a crisis hits so that nothing falls through the cracks.

Warner was principal of a large high school in a district that gives the principal a good deal of autonomy. Consequently, when a crisis hit, he was left to deal with it on his own. Warner had 25 years of goodwill built up as principal of Fargo South, and his partners cut him a lot of slack, undoubtedly believing that he had the matter under control. A new principal may not have been given that much credit. A new principal may have been expected by the principal's Partners to be much more forthcoming with information about events in the school before they had to hear it from the rumor mill.

In the next story, the central office is a pivotal partner in the crisis management plan of the middle school. Although the central office involvement makes sense for overall efficiency, as the story makes clear, nothing replaces the one-on-one communication between the school principal and the parents during a school emergency.

A Crisis in Retrospect

The last thing a principal needs on the morning of the last day of the school year is someone shouting about a kid in the office with a bandana over his face and a rifle in his hands. However, what about the same principal, on the same closing day of school, having to listen to a mother shouting at him because he did not call her and tell her that her daughter, a student at his school, was safe and sound throughout the crisis?

Keeping students safe is absolutely the most important thing school principals do. Fortunately, they have gotten pretty good at it. Assuring parents of this fact, however, is a whole different challenge. Principals may need a little work in the assurance area.

If there is one principal who can give lessons on both topics, it is middle school principal William Bixby of Prince William County Public Schools in suburban Washington, D.C. His last day of school was Friday, June 18, 2004. Nobody panicked when a 12-year-old student, dressed completely in camouflage gear and wearing a red bandana mask, walked into his outer office just after 8:30 a.m. carrying a loaded 30.06 rifle. When he ordered the assembled employees, parents, and students to "get down," they did.

Administrators and staff at the 1,100-student Bull Run Middle School in a northern Virginia suburb had been through numerous emergency drills. What school has not since Columbine? The drills paid off that morning. Assistant Principal Jamie Addington promptly called 911 and began alerting school personnel. Bixby made an announcement over the school loudspeaker initiating a schoolwide "lockdown." Teachers immediately shut off the lights in their classrooms, locked their doors, and got their students under their desks.

Emergency Plan Up to Date

Bixby did not need to consult the Prince William County Public School Emergency Plan that takes up a couple of binders in his office. He was already familiar with it, having worked on it with the district's director of risk management and security to modify it for Bull Run's particular needs. Although the specifics of the plan are revealed only to those who need to know, everybody at Bull Run who needs to know does. Bixby called the central office, alerting them to the situation. Then he left his office through a window with a school roster under his arm.

By then, the police had arrived and, following a crisis plan of their own, moved into the school. Five officers confronted the 12-year-old student and talked him into putting his rifle down. The worst of the crisis was over. At the time, however, nobody could be sure of that. So it was still going to be a long day for Bixby, his staff, students, and their parents scattered at nearby homes and at job sites throughout the metropolitan Washington, D.C., area. The parents were only just learning about a person with a gun in their children's school.

Following procedure, as soon as the police had the student under arrest, they moved carefully through the school classroom by classroom to ensure there was not anyone else with a gun in the building. It was not until later that police identified another student as a coconspirator in the plot to frighten or kill students but who had decided not to go through with it the morning of the episode. As classrooms were cleared by the police, the students and teachers were escorted out of the school and onto waiting buses, where they were moved to another district school. From there, parents were allowed to meet with them.

From a school safety perspective, everything worked perfectly. Nobody was hurt, the building went into lockdown without a hitch, police moved in quickly and efficiently, the building was cleared, and students were moved without any problems. The only glitch? Some parents felt uninformed and were upset about it.

Prince William County Public Schools is a district that takes parent and community relations seriously. A visit to its Web site demonstrates this fact. It is user-friendly, chock full of helpful links, timely information, and plenty of easy-to-access ties to administrative and school sites. The school's Web sites are equally welcoming. Bull Run's Web site is impressive, with regularly updated messages from Principal Bixby directed to parents and community members regarding news about the school. The principal's messages also suggest that the parents and community are integral partners in what goes on at the school. Obviously, schools in Prince William are fairly transparent places; the parents have a good idea about what is going on in them, both good and bad.

Therefore, the district does not sugarcoat the fact that it is located near Washington, D.C., and constantly must be attentive to all kinds of threats, including homeland security alerts. The district's Web site prominently displays a brochure that details what the district intends to do if a crisis occurs. The brochure also states how the public can get information in the event of an emergency.

Planning Fell a Little Short

That is where all the best planning for what happened at Bull Run, when put to the test, fell a little short. Superintendent Kelly said to the *Washington Post* the day after the student walked into the principal's office with the rifle that "the big thing we need to do is find a better way of communicating with parents."

Parents heard about the incident primarily from news accounts or from family or neighbors who picked up the story from radio or television. These early news reports, of course, were sketchy, and the school was not answering its phone for obvious reasons.

Police had blocked all the streets leading to the school, so parents could not get anywhere near the building. When the 12-year-old was in custody, and the drama appeared to be winding down, parents still could not approach the school. Had they tried, they would simply have seen their children being put on buses and transported away.

Superintendent Kelly understands that it is perfectly natural for parents to want to rush to the school to protect their children. Of course, that would just create chaos for the police and for the school staff. As with many districts, when a school goes into a lockdown situation, they need to sort out who belongs in that school and who does not and then empty the school, transferring students by bus to another school to be picked up by parents and relatives so that they can search for anyone left who does not belong.

How this all works is detailed in district pamphlets handed out to parents at the start of school and made available throughout the year on the district's Web site. In these materials, the district reminds parents that in the event of a crisis, they should turn to the Web site.

In this instance, the Web site was a good place for parents to find information. In fact, as soon as the district office received word of the crisis at Bull Run, it had a message on the district Web site alerting parents and community members to the situation and directing their attention to the "crisis/emergency preparedness" brochure. A quick read of that brochure would alert a parent that the best way to obtain information about the unfolding crisis would be to

- Monitor the district's Web site;
- Check the district's information line;
- Listen to local radio and television station broadcasts;
- Use the school telephone trees; and
- Use the e-notification system that had been developed.

The brochure closed by stating, "Don't call the school." Part of the problem, it was discussed in the aftermath, is that the school's telephone tree is triggered by an autodialer system that sends out a message to all the parents maintained on it. The system resides in the school, however, which was vacated on orders of the police; nobody was allowed back in for several hours.

Principal Moved Quickly

Prince William County Schools did not waste any time after the event to restore communication links, and nobody moved more quickly than Bull Run Principal Bixby. The next day, Saturday, he opened the school to allow students in to pick up their backpacks and report cards and to talk to counselors. Parents were welcome too. Many of them came. Nineteen students signed up for formal counseling, and many more spoke to counselors informally.

On Monday, Bixby posted a letter to the "Bull Run Family" on the school's Web site, telling it how proud he was of its response to that day's events: "Our students and staff demonstrated composure, compassion, and bravery; we are truly blessed," he wrote. He announced that a school-community information meeting would be held within 3 days at the school involving district officials and local police: "All your questions will be answered," he promised.

At that event, parents and community members gave both the principal and the police standing ovations. Some concerns were expressed, to be sure, but mostly the crowd was grateful.

Two weeks later, with the help of the school's PTA, Bixby threw a well-attended party at the school for the students and staff. The attendance exceeded everyone's expectations and drew considerable media attention. "We had a really good year," he told the *Washington Post*, "and we have good kids. We wanted to have a positive closure for them."

By the time the party occurred, Bixby was able to assure parents that the school staff had figured out how to operate the telephone tree remotely. (A version of this story appeared in an article in *Principal* magazine, March-April, 2005, authored by Joe Schneider.)

Principal Bixby reinforces the principle of communication management that it is built on trust and respect. From a bureaucratic standpoint, he had all his communication bases covered. The parents had been told numerous times how to obtain information in the event of a crisis. When the crisis unfolded, however, Bixby realized that the formal communication processes in place were insufficient because they did not give his key stakeholder groups—his students and their parents—an opportunity to ask questions and to seek reassurance. His willingness to bring the parents and the children back together on two different occasions soon after the event demonstrated his leadership skills and united his active publics on his behalf. The two events also generated considerable media attention in the community, thus creating a positive image for Bixby and the school among other stakeholder groups in the broader community. The major point here is that the transparent school environment at Bull Run, characterized by use of the symmetric communication model by Principal Bixby, enabled him to turn a school violence situation into a major public relations win for the school.

Putting It All Together: Using the Tools to Move "Aware" Parents to "Active" Parents

As discussed in previous chapters, every principal deals with two groups of parents. The active group processes information that comes from the school, seeks out the principal when they have questions, gets involved when problems or issues arise, and actively participates in school-related activities. The aware group is involved with the school because their children attend. They may not be active yet for a variety of reasons (e.g., new to the community, long working hours, language or cultural differences, and distrust of government agencies). In some cases, they are simply waiting to be asked.

In other words, the parents constitute an aware public for a school principal. That is, they certainly are aware that their children attend school. They know they should be involved in their child's education, and most would like to be there. For a variety of reasons, however, they are not. They may process information that is brought home by the student but not necessarily follow up on it. They seldom seek out information about their children's education, either because they are not invited or because they do not know the questions to ask. Consequently, their children's education suffers, the principal is frustrated, and the reciprocal communication from the school to these parents is nonexistent.

Galen Hoffstadt, principal of Luther Jones Elementary School in Corpus Christi Independent School District in Texas, was one of those frustrated principals and knew she had to get parents and the entire community involved, in anything and everything that had to do with the school, and increase their interest and lower any barriers they have erected to active participation in their children's education.

Luther Jones Elementary is a neighborhood school that also serves a very large military population and consequently has a high turnover of students and parents. The parents come from all over the world, from different types of schools, from different cultures, and from different religious backgrounds. They may not have been actively involved in their children's previous schools. They may not speak English as a first language.

Principal Initiates Plan

The strategic communication plan for moving parents from aware to an active public begins at Luther Jones Elementary School in early July when Mrs. Hoffstadt returns to work for the start of the new school year. She is in the office and she is answering her own phone, which frequently surprises most parents.

She always uses her first name. She never mentions that she is the principal, unless asked, and she never says anything about being the National Distinguished Principal of Texas.

The first "ice-breaking" activity to move parents from an aware to active public occurs on the day students register for school. The event takes place approximately 2 weeks before school starts. The principal, her administrative team, the 36-member executive committee of the PTA, and parent volunteers are all prepped and ready to begin recruiting the new parents the minute the doors swing open.

The rules require the parents to register their children on-site, so when both parents live at home, they usually both show up. The main event occurs in the cafeteria. Each grade has a separate table staffed by two or three parents whose children attended that grade the previous year. The PTA has the job of recruiting the parents to staff the tables. Hoffstadt focuses on using skills that most would expect to see at a retail store—everyone smiling, pleasant greetings, and tours of the building.

When the teachers return to school during the first week of August, the PTA hosts a breakfast. Both parents and teachers take this opportunity to mingle before the school year becomes hectic.

The day before the first day of school, Hoffstadt makes another effort to move the parents from aware to active status and to make them a permanent part of her active stakeholders group, the volunteers in public schools. Parents of new kindergarten students and the youngsters attend what is called "Kindercamp." Kindercamp is a must-attend session for all new kindergarten students, their parents, and any extended family members who live with the students and may on occasion pick them up or drop them off at school.

At Kindercamp, family members and the children meet with their teachers for 15 minutes. Then, Hoffstadt greets the visitors using the public address system. She then invites the adults in the family to the cafeteria, leaving the students with their teachers. For approximately 1 hour and 45 minutes, Hoffstadt explains how the school works, the rules and regulations, and her expectations for parents and students for the year. She also tells parents more about herself, her distinguished career, and her family, and she reassures parents how committed she is to each and every student and their safety. In addition, Hoffstadt mentions the many awards the school has received, including recognition as a National PTA School of Excellence for 2004–2007 because of outstanding parental involvement. That, of course, gives her an opportunity to introduce the PTA officers who are there to sign up parents for a variety of assignments and volunteer opportunities.

Students Receive Agenda Planners

To keep parents involved and informed, as well as help students stay organized, every child in the school is given an "agenda planner" on the first day of class. It looks like an adult's organizer or day timer. The agenda planner has a pocket in the front and contains everything students need to remember about their schedule for the year, including the yearly calendar, homework assignments, field trip reminders, and daily activities.

To keep the parents involved, the teachers require "scholars" (Hoffstadt refers to her students as scholars) to have at least one parent initial the agenda planner every school night. This increases the likelihood that the parent has also read the agenda planner and is aware of the nightly homework assignment, upcoming field trip, projects, the science fair, or behavior issues that need to be addressed. Teachers communicate positive comments during the first 2 weeks of school.

The front flap on the planner is designed to carry notes home from the principal and the scholar's teacher. At least once a week, it contains a formal newsletter from the principal. The flap can also be used to carry notes from the parent back to the principal and to her advisory committee, the Planning and Decision-Making Team. The team consists of teachers, administrators, the counselor, special education resource specialists, PTA officers, two business members, two parent members, and two community members who do not have children attending the school.

Encouraging the kindergarten parents to go from aware to active status is scarcely a challenge for Hoffstadt. She also opens the doors for what the school calls the "meet the teacher" program. This is designed for the parents of students entering Grades 1 through 5. This group contains additional newcomers to the school, including some parents with a history of passive involvement with their children's education. They are encouraged to get involved from the first minute they step through the door.

They arrive, along with the veterans of the system, and go door to door looking for the names of their children posted outside the classrooms. Once the names are located, the children and their family members gather with the teachers in the correct rooms to get acquainted. The students' names are on the desks, along with school materials they will need during the first week of class.

Forty-five minutes later, Hoffstadt makes her welcoming announcement and calls the adults and the families new to the school to the cafeteria to "meet the principal." Meanwhile, other parents are recruited by PTA executive committee members to add their names to the many sign-up sheets for the various activities being planned for the school year.

Hoffstadt does not stop her efforts there. The school's next opportunity to solicit parental involvement is during the first PTA meeting and the first parents-only open house during the second week of school. During the open house, the teachers and the PTA members explain to the parents how much they are needed to ensure the education of their children and the smooth operation of the school.

"Doughnuts With Dads"

Once she has gotten parents involved, Hoffstadt continues to solicit more parents, more community members, and more involvement. The goal is to expose every parent to opportunities that might connect to their interests. She keeps a steady stream of activities coming at the parents through the year (e.g., "muffins with moms" and "doughnuts with dads," which both bring parents into the school for breakfast with their scholars, and "chilifest," a tailgate party that attracts 2,500 family members for a luncheon, chili contest, and games).

In addition, Hoffstadt is in constant communication with parents, and so are the teachers. In addition to the newsletter from the principal every Monday, parents receive regular notes from teachers about individual students. Knowing this, parents check their youngsters' agenda planners daily. The school also maintains an active Web site. The PTA executive committee meets with the principal monthly for approximately 3 hours on average, and the agenda covers a wide range of topics. The Planning and Decision-Making Team meets monthly, and although it primarily focuses on student achievement, the group does consider every issue that comes to its attention from parents.

Hoffstadt's efforts have been successful. Luther Jones Elementary School has been selected by the Texas Education Agency as a Pathfinder Collaborative School. That means during any given year, hundreds of teachers and administrators from across Texas visit the school to find out how it obtains high achievement scores. The school is known for its accelerated curriculum enrichment program for gifted and talented children as well as its special communication and physical needs program for children with severe disabilities.

Principal Hoffstadt does an excellent job of reaching out to new stakeholders and inducting them into an active public in support of their children's education and, in the process, Luther Jones Elementary School. She has found throughout the years that this recruitment effort takes leadership, the buy-in of her staff and a host of PTA volunteers, and many different gimmicks (e.g., feeding the dads seems to be helpful). The point is that she is willing to do whatever it takes to increase parents' involvement in the education of their children. What binds the effort together is Principal Hoffstadt's incredible communication management skills. She understands stakeholders, knows her publics, and has refined involvement to an art form.

Summary

This chapter featured three case studies and attempted to drive home three messages. First, principals who operate transparent schools that rely on symmetric communication models tend to have an advantage during times of crisis because they have built up the respect and trust of their Partners. Second, establishing and maintaining effective partnerships is the principals' responsibility and it is a lot of work, but the payoffs are worth it. Third, the principal needs a plan in place that defines how he will regularly communicate with Partners as well as how he intends to communicate with them in times of crisis (e.g., snow day, school closing, and health alert). The plan needs to be up-to-date and well understood by all the parties involved, including those who will rely on it for information.

6

Communicating Under Pressure

Most of this book has focused on the principal's need to manage the communication from the school to its various stakeholder publics. Occasionally, however, principals will probably have to cope with one-way communication coming at them from very well-organized groups that want to persuade the principals to change their behaviors or attitudes or both. Sometimes, these groups will be outsiders or nonstakeholders and thus tempting to ignore. More often, they will be made up of stakeholders organized into active publics that will quote federal statutes, enlist the backing of well-financed special-interest groups, and employ some of the best legal minds in the community. Their issue may be the teaching of evolution, sex education, the role of religion in the classroom, or any of a dozen hot-button topics. The point is that when these groups are in the principal's office for a showdown, they will be armed with strong opinions, legal backing, and the financial support to take their cause to the next level if need be. Such situations will test the communication management skills of even the best school administrator.

At other times, principals are going to have to communicate during times of crisis. Normally placid stakeholders typically defined as latent publics all of a sudden become aware publics demanding information about the school and its treatment of its students. If the information does not come fast enough, or if it is not sufficient, the aware publics can easily become active publics in opposition to the principals' efforts to provide leadership during the crisis. Even a principal's normally solid supporters—her active public of partners—will only stay with her so long before they too become actively hostile if they are dissatisfied with the quality and quantity of information they receive during a crisis. In other words, nothing quite tests the communication management skills of a principal like a crisis.

During a time of crisis, stakeholders of all kinds are in an aware public mode in that they are seeking information from as many sources as possible: the principal, of course, but also the media, the neighbors, their children, classroom teachers, and Web sites. The principal may well be the most trusted source of information, but if he is not able to provide current and complete information, the public will turn to other sources. If these sources seem to be more complete and comprehensive, they could satisfy the public's need for information, even if it is wrong and counter to the best interests of the school. In fact, these sources could result in an active public forming because of the information they receive. When that happens, the stakeholders will likely only process information that reinforces their belief about what they know about the situation at the school. When the principal attempts to explain the situation later, it will fall on deaf ears because the stakeholders will have already made up their minds about what happened at the school.

The point is that during a crisis, it is critical for the principal to communicate frequently and honestly with his key stakeholders about events as they are occurring because in today's breaking news environment, if he does not, somebody else will.

IDEA Legislation Creates Active Public

Active publics can form around just about any issue imaginable before marching into the principal's office for a confrontation. Perhaps no active public tests the communication skills of a principal quite like advocates for students with disabilities. What should be a caring conversation about the needs of students with disabilities can quickly deteriorate into a heated exchange about whose reading of state and federal law and regulations is more accurate and whose legal counsel is better informed.

What makes the conversations regarding children with disabilities so difficult is that everyone prefaces their opening salvo by saying they are only there to argue for what is best for the children. They all sincerely believe that to be the case. The problem is that everything possible cannot be done with the resources the parents and the school have available. Then, the disagreements begin to creep into the discussion.

The principals say the schools are doing all they can; the parents say that is not sufficient or that what the schools provide falls short of what the law requires. Then the principals explain their reading of the law, and the parents explain their reading of the law. Then the special education directors are called in, and the parents bring in their special education advocates and perhaps attorneys. The districts respond with their attorneys. Soon, the principals and the parents are not the principal discussants. Nuances of the law, interpretations of regulations, and precedents established over time are thrown on the table. Somebody threatens that they may have to go to court. Somebody counters by suggesting that they may be happier in a private school.

That is when principals have to ask themselves what they could have done to prevent this from happening. Well, perhaps nothing. At some point, however, before the lawyers and advocacy groups got involved, the parents of the children with the disabilities were an aware public searching for information about their children's education at the local school.

Aware publics are a principal's major challenge. A principal does not know when they are forming and can hardly be expected to know all the issues that they are looking into. If an aware public searches for information about the principal's school and does not find it, however, the search does not stop. The aware public will keep searching. The problem is that it will settle for whatever information it can find from second-hand sources. Then it will morph into an active public using the information it received from what the principal may well consider to be less than reliable sources. Had an aware public come to the principal for information, he just may have been able to provide what it needed.

Parents with a child with a disability should be able to locate on the school district's Web site considerable information about what they can expect when they enroll their child in the district's schools. There should be all kinds of information that can be downloaded, links to other Web sites that can be accessed, and phone numbers of district personnel who can be called directly with questions. Before the child ever appears in the school, his or her parents should know exactly what to expect from the district. In other words, the kind of dispute described previously would never occur, or if it did, it would take place in a district official's office before the start of school and it would not involve the school principal.

If a dispute occurs after the start of school, by then the parents and the child are members of the principal's partnership, as are the special education teacher and specialists that assist the child. Perhaps it can be resolved by a partnership committee. It if appears to be an interpretation of the child's rights under provisions of the Individuals with Disabilities Education Act (IDEA), then the principal can move the discussion into her office and assemble the district personnel required to settle the matter as quickly as possible, keeping in mind that the child's interests are her interests. That is, the principal's job is to maintain the trust and respect of her fellow partnership members; she should let the central office officials carry the fight for the district. Win or lose, the principal is going to want to retain a good relationship with the Partners.

Of course, the dispute over the child with disabilities does not originate from the principal's office. The principal owes it to her partnership to be well versed on the requirements of IDEA, to have a good working relationship with her district's and school's special education administrators, and to be sensitive to the special-interest lobbies that champion the cause of the disabled. The best protection that principals have against a negative IDEA active public is to discourage one from ever forming, which is done by eliminating the fuel that a negative active public feeds on.

If the parents of children with disabilities know they can get immediate access to all the information they need about their rights from their school's Web site, they will have less need to search elsewhere. If these parents can get answers they can rely on from special education administrators within the principal's district and school, they will have less need to seek out advocacy groups and legal counsel. If these parents are part of the principal's active partnership and believe that the teachers and administrators have created a family-like school, and the school is located in a caring community, then chances are the parents will believe that the school is an important part of their life too. In other words, the trick is to create a positive IDEA active public within the school's partnership and to nurture it.

Principals need to be vigilant to changes in the law and new rules and regulations from federal and state agencies. When this happens, advocacy organizations and attorneys who specialize in special education law bombard parents of children with disabilities with e-mails and fliers about "how to advocate for your child."

The principal needs to give up-to-date information about changes affecting the children to the parents before anyone else does. The first message should state that "changes are coming" and give the parents advance notice about what is causing the changes, such as the reauthorization of federal legislation. Principals need to let them know what Web sites to monitor if they wish to follow along as the school leaders will be doing. Then principals should inform them when the bill has passed and tell them what the district's special education administrators think it means. Parents should be alerted as to when there will be new rules and regulations, and these should be shared as soon as they are available. Principals should give their partners an e-mail alert 1 or 2 days before the regulations are available to the general public. They may get the regulations from a dozen sources the same day they get them from principals. They are likely to pay attention to the notice from the principals, however. If they have concerns, the principals will be the ones they will go to for clarification. That is called "keeping it in the family." That is providing leadership. That is communication management.

The Federal Government Provides Funds and Mandates

The granddaddy of all federal legislation is the Elementary and Secondary Education Act (ESEA) passed by Congress in 1965. Among other things, it funds Title I, the major piece of federal legislation that addresses the needs of economically disadvantaged children. At the end of the 20th century, spending for Title I had increased to more than $8 billion per year. Many members of Congress wondered if the money was being well spent. Fiscal conservatives kept showing a chart that appeared to indicate that as federal spending increased, student test scores declined. Educational interest groups, however, argued that Title I was underfunded and that more money was needed if all the eligible economically disadvantaged students were to be served. The tug back and forth heightened as ESEA came up for reauthorization in 2001. The White House and both the House and the Senate were under Republican control, something that had not happened in all the years since ESEA originally passed. Clearly, the time was ripe for a major overhaul of the legislation.

The conservatives in Congress wanted a bill that would create vouchers. The liberals who still believed they "owned" the bill wanted a rewrite that would force accountability on the schools to increase achievement for poor and minority children or risk losing federal funds. The liberals did not want the risk to include giving the money away to parents for use in private or parochial schools, however. The education interest groups, mostly cut out of the debate, stood off to the side and raised their voices for "more money." It was a comfortable cheer for the interest groups—one they had been carrying on with success for more than 30 years.

The resulting legislation caught the interest groups by surprise. Although it did indeed have more money than previous versions of ESEA, it also represented a bargain struck between conservative Republicans and liberal Democrats. In exchange for no vouchers, Congress came up with a bill that was heavy on accountability and high on expectations for student achievement. This bill became the No Child Left Behind Act of 2001 (NCLB).

The law is much too complicated to discuss here, but principals unfamiliar with it should study it by accessing any one of a dozen Web sites (www.ed.gov/nclb). The bill involves every state and practically all the school districts in the country, as long as the districts accept federal funds to help balance state and local spending.

The law requires schools to have "highly qualified teachers." It is difficult to fault this requirement. The teacher must hold at least a bachelor's degree and have passed a state test of content knowledge. Elementary teachers must demonstrate that they know how to teach reading and mathematics. Teachers in higher grades must demonstrate knowledge of the subject they teach or have at least majored in that subject.

Paraprofessionals who assist teachers in Title I schools must have completed 2 years of college or be able to pass a test that assesses their ability to support their teacher in reading, writing, and math instruction. This is a controversial provision. Many paraprofessionals in Title I schools do not have 2 years of college education. Many are there because they are facile in one or more languages; that is, they speak the language of many of the students in the classroom. It is likely that the classroom teachers do not. What worried members of Congress, however, is that studies have shown that many of these paraprofessionals were actually teaching youngsters in their native language. This raised the obvious question: Was the teacher supervising the teaching when she could not understand what was being said? Members of Congress decided that if the paraprofessionals are going to be teaching, they should at least have 2 years of college education.

The law states that parents have the right to know if their child is attending a school where the teacher is not qualified or the paraprofessional lacks the 2-year certification. In addition, the school has to inform the parents of the scores of the new statewide tests for the school as a whole. The school also has to inform the parents of the test scores broken out into four subgroups:

Children with disabilities

Children with limited English proficiency

Racial minorities

Children from low-income families

Beginning in 2005, every school must test all children in Grades 3 through 8 every year in math and science, and by 2007 they must be tested in science as well. These test scores will determine if a school is making what is known as "adequate yearly progress" (AYP) toward the goal of proficiency for all children by the 2013–2014 deadline. Proficiency means that every child is performing at the average grade level. What makes it challenging is the fact that all four subgroups of children, as well as the school as a whole, must meet the AYP goal or the school will fail.

A principal of a Title I school labeled "failing" because it did not meet its AYP goal for any of the subgroups for 2 consecutive years must inform parents of children attending that school that they may choose to attend a nonfailing school in that school district. If all the schools in that district failed, the child has the option of using district money to attend a school in another district.

If the Title I school is a failing school for 3 consecutive years, then it must provide "supplemental services" to the children still enrolled, including tutoring, afterschool programs, and summer school. The state department of education determines who is eligible to provide the services, but the district pays for the cost of providing them.

If a school has not satisfactorily met its AYP goal for 4 consecutive years, the principal is expected to replace staff and try a new curriculum, reorganize its management structure, and even hire outside experts. The reason is simple: If things have not improved by the following year, the school district will be expected to replace the principal and the staff. The school may well open up again as a charter school under the management of a private firm. If all else fails, the state will take over the management of the school.

That, in brief, is the NCLB legislation, and its passage was greeted with mixed emotions by educators. Congress did boost spending for Title I with NCLB's passage, and vouchers were put on the back burner for the time being, both positive outcomes in a Republican-controlled Congress. The accountability provisions were ratcheted up quite a bit, but many in both parties believed that too many schools had not been meeting the needs of poor and minority students.

Clearly, Congress had to signal that it was not just going to hand over Title I money in the same old "business as usual" mode.

Undoubtedly, Congress will make some corrections in the law when it comes up for reauthorization in 2007. Some things are unlikely to change, however. First, the public is going to continue to expect to see test scores broken down by schools and by subgroups within schools. Second, the public is going to expect schools to have quality teachers and paraprofessionals and to be required to report publicly when they do not. Third, the public is going to expect schools to provide supplementary schools and options for other schools when they cannot meet the grade themselves, which means that the schools are going to be much more open about how they operate and why.

Ambushing the NCLB Active Public

Previously, it was shown how a hostile IDEA active public can go after the school principal. A hostile NCLB active public is lurking out there too. A variety of advocacy groups are trying to mobilize parents into forming hostile active publics to march into the principal's office and demand their rights under the laws of the NCLB. One of them is Joyce L. Epstein, head of the National Network of Partnership Schools at Johns Hopkins University.

Epstein, a heroine in a previous chapter in this book, is mentioned here to suggest that the advocacy groups stirring up parents on behalf of NCLB are not enemies of good schools. What Epstein and colleagues are trying to do is alert parents of children in desperate situations that they do not have to take it anymore, and they should not.

Of course, some of the recipients of these broadsides are going to be confused and think there is a problem with their children's school too. That might bring them to a school that is doing fine. The principal of that school might not appreciate Dr. Epstein's suggestion that parents of his students visit his office and use her checklist of questions to inquire about the school's progress under NCLB. Many principals are going to be uncomfortable with an office full of parents holding checklists, but parents have rights and increasingly more of them are starting to realize it. It will be another test of a principal's communication management skills.

The solution for principals, of course, is first and foremost to do good work. Then communicate about it. If the reader skipped Chapter 4, now would be a good time to revisit it. If the school leader has a school-family-community partnership operating in her school, she is already engaging faculty, staff, parents, students, and community groups in six types of involvement. One of these is communicating. Every member of the partnership should be familiar with most of the school's programs, policies, test scores, and politics.

In other words, when NCLB became law, the partnership would have done a quick inventory to determine if any of its faculty and paraprofessionals needed to do anything to meet the federal qualifications to hold their positions. If they did, then they would have received the training or people with the requirements would have been moved into their positions.

The test scores would have been disaggregated and studied carefully by the entire partnership. If a subgroup was not making its AYP, the partnership's action team would have assigned a committee the task of determining why. When they had an answer, they would have moved quickly to address the problem so that the test scores would improve the following year. Even if the test scores never met the federal requirements, the partnership would have known that it was addressing the problem and making progress. The parents of the children involved would have known it too. When they contemplated their options, including changing schools, they could have asked themselves if they thought their children would be better served by the receiving school than the one they were leaving.

The point is that as a principal practicing the two-way symmetric model of communication, information is shared as a tool to be used by the partnership for problem solving. Every Partner knows the NCLB requirements. The school does not make a secret of it. There is no "you versus us" with the law in the middle.

The principal involves the partnership in the operation of the school so they understand what AYP means. They know what a qualified teacher is because they know their children's teachers personally. A principal can talk about "federal definitions" of qualified teachers and the stakeholders do not confuse it with the real meaning of qualified teachers. The same can be said about "federal definitions" of qualified paraprofessionals or adequate yearly progress: There is the federal definition and what the stakeholders agree it is.

As a consequence of NCLB, principals need to be concerned about the provision that allows parents to request that their children be moved to another school in the district if their school is low performing. Principals are probably going to want their action committees to set up a committee to determine how best to integrate all the new families that will want to enroll during the next few years.

A Crisis May Never Occur, but What if it Does?

Although crises are frequently shocking when reported on the news, a typical thought is, "That wouldn't happen to me." Principals, district offices, parents, and communities are still reflecting on and preparing for crises that were once unimaginable—for example, September 11, 2001, or, to bring it closer to home, the tragedy at Columbine or the 2005 shootings at Red Lake in northern Minnesota. At one time, these events were unthinkable. Today, crises not only include the gun or knife in the backpack or drugs in the school locker, but they also include tornados, flash floods, hurricanes, and terrorist alerts.

The key to crisis prevention is that in the past several years schools and districts have become better prepared for the unthinkable. It is the rare district, regardless of location or size, that does not have a reasonable crisis plan in place and coordinated with local police and fire departments. Typically, these plans consist of a written document in a three-ring binder that includes checklists, contact information, step-by-step guidelines, and fact sheets. It is not a public document, but everyone who needs access to it has access.

The district generally takes responsibility for preparing the crisis management plan for the schools. The principals are but cogs in the larger system and are expected to play a particular role according to the plan. Obviously, they are responsible for the safety of the people in their own building, and that takes precedence over everything else. What generally happens in a crisis is that the concern for safety blocks out the concern for communication, which, in turn, can create serious problems for the principal. Those who look to the principal for leadership expect safety to be the highest priority, of course, but they also expect to be kept informed about what is happening. Parents and others who care for the students want to know about their status from minute to minute. It is not a request for information; it is a demand. A principal who does not anticipate being able to respond to this demand risks being judged an ineffective leader.

Therefore, as part of the crisis plan, principals need to ensure that the district provides upfront for multiple ways by which key stakeholders (i.e., parents and other family members) can be kept informed about the crisis and its impact on the conditions in the school and the children enrolled there. Box 6.1 is an example of a crisis plan from the Georgia Emergency Management Agency.

Box 6.1   Preparing for an Emergency

- A school spokesperson should be designated for the crisis site. This person should be familiar with the school's safety plan.
- A public information officer should be designated to assist the school spokesperson in facilitating media inquiries.
- Fax numbers for local media need to be programmed into the school's fax machine.
- Media contact numbers should be placed in the Emergency Evacuation Kit.
- A media staging area needs to be determined. The site should provide a good camera view of the school, yet be located away from response operations, the incident command center, and the family unification site.
- A location for media briefings needs to be chosen.
- Fact sheets with background information about the school must be created.
- School personnel need to meet with local media representatives to discuss ways that the media can support crisis response efforts. Schools may want to conduct training to acquaint administrators with the process of making statements during a crisis.
- A system is in place to post updated press releases on the school's Web site during a crisis.

Provided by the School Safety Project of the Georgia Emergency Management Agency
1–800-TRY-GEMA www.gema.state.ga.us

Before a crisis occurs, it is wise to communicate with stakeholders. Principals should encourage key publics to download the parent's guide to emergencies through e-mail, newsletters, and notes sent home with students. Even if parents do not review the school's handbook, there at least has been some communication on where to find the information when it is necessary. Supplying this information in a hard copy and via e-mail is also important.

A principal's role in a crisis is vast. As the leader of the school, his or her most important role is to ensure everyone's safety, specifically the children in the school but also teachers, staff, volunteers, and visitors. Once everyone has been evacuated and the building has been secured, the principal needs to act as the key communicator. Just as the school has a written crisis plan that includes how to evacuate the building, what do to during a lockdown, and how to respond to a bomb threat, an action plan for communication should also be part of the initial plan.

The district crisis plan may already include a communication plan, but it behooves principals to carefully review the suggested steps and enhance them in accordance with the individual principal's partnership. Steps on how to communicate internally are probably already outlined in the plan, but principals should review these guidelines regularly, particularly whenever a new administrator or support staff member joins the team. When a crisis occurs, the principal will realize that the job of communicating with the various publics is more than the principal can do on his or her own (see the case study of the Fargo, North Dakota, principal in Chapter 5).

The key issue for principals is how to send accurate and timely information to stakeholders. Part of a principal's crisis communication plan should include proactive communication with key stakeholders. This includes multiple communication mediums because during a crisis, no one medium can be considered solely reliable. Telephones and cell phones, Web sites, e-mails, fliers and memos, and a strategic use of the media are a principal's basic tools.

What should a principal do when a crisis occurs? See When a Crisis Happens (Box 6.2) for the basic steps to follow. In addition, a principal's school plan should include all the "what-ifs" for the communication team. Because the school's Web site is a key communication tool, someone should be available to update the site with the most current information available. If a phone tree or e-mail system is in place, it requires a procedure to activate it quickly. Principals need to consider that their most carefully constructed plan can run into problems. (See the case study of the Prince William principal in Chapter 5). Finally, principals need to know the next steps to follow.

Box 6.2   When a Crisis Happens

- *Do not go it alone.* The principal should work out in advance with the key staff what tasks each member should perform. Then, when the crisis occurs, they should be assigned to take responsibility for those tasks. The principal needs to know he cannot do it all alone and that he has his back covered. Others in positions of authority should be involved from the start, and they need to know they have the authority to act.

- *Understand the circumstances.* Everyone needs to fight the temptation to "tell the story" before all the facts are known. School officials should pass on only what is known for sure. They should not hesitate to say, "I don't know and I will have to get back to you when I learn the facts to answer that question." Then they should make a note of the question and attempt to obtain an answer and respond as soon as possible. They should not spread hearsay or inaccurate information.

- *Inform the central office.* The principal needs to involve the central office as soon as a crisis occurs in his school. Generally, the district's crisis manual has a procedure for doing this. Even without a procedure, the first call after police/ fire/ambulance should be to the central office to alert the superintendent's office. That office can then notify the appropriate district officials within the central office as to who needs to be involved (e.g., building and grounds, maintenance, community relations, and school safety).

- *Communicate.* The principal needs to keep a constant line of communication open to staff, students, and parents. Principals today need to realize that increasingly more students carry cell phones and consequently anything said to them about a crisis within the school is going to be conveyed to parents and family members outside the school within minutes after the principal finishes talking. So the principal has little time between notifying his internal audience and his external audiences about the situation.

(Continued)

Box 6.2 (Continued)

- *Inform parents.* The principal needs a plan developed in advance to notify parents. In many districts, parents will want to be called on their cell phones. If the crisis is located at the school, a telephone tree may be activated that would alert parents by calling their cell phones and directing their attention to a school Web site that has more detailed information. If the crisis is broader than the school, cell phones may not work and other methods may have to be relied on, such as calls to local all-news radio and television stations as a first alert. The message should be to direct the parents to a prearranged site where they can receive information about how to access information about where they could go to pick up their child in the event the school had to be evacuated.

- *Keep the community informed.* The district and the principal should work out in advance who has the overall responsibility for communicating with the media and the community at large. In larger districts, the communication relations department will probably assume that responsibility. In a small district, the superintendent might well be on the scene and handle it. In rare cases, the principal will be expected to be the district's spokesperson. Generally, the principal will be given the task of working with his school's key stakeholders while the district assigns someone the responsibility for communicating with the broader stakeholder audience. Obviously, the principal and the district spokesperson have to work as a team to ensure close coordination of message.

Technology and a Crisis

On September 11, 2001, in both New York City and Washington, D.C., cell phones, as well as landline phones, were essentially useless. The authors' attempt to reach one another by phone, even though they lived only 50 miles apart, failed. Throughout the nation, attempts to log onto Web sites to get the most current information were fruitless because of the surge in Internet traffic. The point is that although communication technology tools will help principals communicate effectively during a crisis, several communication mediums should be included when planning for a crisis. Furthermore, the principal needs to be able to access these tools inside and outside the school.

Principals need to consider, for example, a bomb threat, when the entire building must be evacuated. Can e-mail still be received and sent on handheld devices? Can the Web site be updated from a mobile device or from the district office? Can phone calls still be made? Principals need to make sure they have the ability to communicate, either individually or with group notifications, in any situation.

During a crisis, the first three questions that parents will ask will be basic: Is my child safe? What is being done at the school? and How do I get to my child? Although they would like all the answers to these questions at once, a principal needs to communicate with parents as soon as possible even if all the answers are not yet available. Through a series of messages, whether they are e-mails, phone messages, or Web site updates, principals and members of the communication team can keep parents updated. That may mean the first message conveys that there has been an incident at the school. The children have been secured, and the school has gone into lockdown. The school communicates that the situation remains under investigation and parents will be informed of its status within the next hour. At that time, they will learn some basic steps for the remainder of the day. The key for principals is to keep a steady stream of information coming from the school to alleviate worries and keep parents, partners, and the district office up-to-date.

The media may be a different story. Because a principal is busy thinking about the safety of the students, faculty, and staff and then communicating with them and parents, talking to a reporter is probably the last thing a principal wants to do during a crisis. Although the principal is still the key communicator for the school and asked to respond to media inquiries after the incident, the district public information staff can play a key role during the height of the crisis by being the central spokespeople.[1]

Generalizations About Active Publics

In this chapter, the focus has been on three active publics: one around IDEA, one around NCLB, and one around family members who have children inside a school undergoing a crisis of some kind. Obviously, many other examples could be used. Principals deal with active publics quite frequently. The parents of cheerleaders, if they have an issue, could emerge as an active public. The men's basketball team and their parents, if the coach quits midseason, might emerge as an active public until the issue is resolved.

Remember the definition of an active public: a group of people who have come to grips with a similar problem or issue, recognized its existence, and organized to do something about it. Generally, an active public is not open to new information, and it only seeks and retains information that reinforces the attitudes and behaviors it has previously chosen.

Being an active public by itself is neither "positive" nor "negative" from the principal's viewpoint. Some of the principal's strongest supporters are going to be partners unified into active publics that he can count on time and time again to be at his side for the good of the school. A strong leader will work to create many active publics in support of his mission.

Occasionally, however, active publics will form in opposition to the principal. The fewer the better, obviously. A skilled principal will work with partners to head off the formation of a negative active public by providing aware publics with the information they need to steer them into positive active publics or to sooth them back to latent status.

The best the principal can do with a hostile active public is to give it a hearing, let it know she understands its position, explain the school's position, ask if it understands its position, and then take some solace in the fact that at least the principal and the active public understand each other's viewpoint.

That may not seem important at the time, but it could be worth a lot later for the simple reason that issues come and go, and the publics that form around them do too. In other words, principals will want the people who come to them as a hostile active public to leave their offices at least knowing they gave them a fair hearing and that the principals understood their viewpoint. This is because the specific issue is not likely to be the sole basis on which they determine their relationship with the school. Another issue will come along, and they will find themselves in another public, maybe one more amenable to the principals' viewpoint.

Note, however, that some people get excited only about one issue. Principals may meet community members because of an issue and then never interact with them again once the issue wanes in intensity.

Summary

In this chapter, school leaders were told that they will be confronted with active publics that want to persuade them to go along with their viewpoint. Active publics can form around just about any issue, and they will do so. School leaders, however, can expect to find active publics already in existence related to children with disabilities and accountability provisions. Also, every school crisis will create an immediate active public.

The best defense against hostile active publics is to get to them before they become active. That is, principals should try to identify aware publics and address their needs before they go elsewhere for information and resolution. Finally, principals need to retain the trust and respect of their stakeholders, even if there is not agreement on all issues.

Note

1. For more detailed discussion on crisis communication and management, review the National School Public Relations Association's *The Complete Crisis Communication Management Manual* (2001) and the National School Safety and Security Web site at www.schoolsecurity.org

7

Thinking Strategically About Communication

Throughout this book, the principal has been portrayed as the manager of communication between the school and its stakeholders. Most of the time, the stakeholders who the principals are most concerned with are their Partners: the faculty, the parents, and the community members who contribute to the school's success. These are the most active stakeholders. Of course, another active stakeholder public is the Enablers, and key among them is the superintendent's office.

In this chapter, the relationship between principals and the superintendent's office is explored further. Obviously, the nature of the relationship will vary from district to district depending to a large extent on the size and complexity of the school system. In a district with one or two schools, the superintendent is likely to pick up the phone and talk casually with the principals who he has probably known personally for years. In a large district, the superintendent probably works with the principals through deputy or assistant superintendents. Nevertheless, one constant is true across every district: The principals are closer to teachers, the parents, and the community members than is the superintendent. When she wants to know what they are thinking, she is wise to ask her building-level administrators for their insights.

Principals Can Use Any of Several Communication Models

Principals are also managers within a larger organizational structure. As such, superintendents frequently call on them to perform as communication links between the district and its external audiences. When performing this communicator role, principals generally use the public information model. That is, they represent the organization's interests. As such, they attempt to convey its viewpoint to the stakeholders in a manner that boosts the image of the district or school or, at a minimum, does nothing to tarnish it in the minds of the people targeted by the communication.

In some cases, principals are asked to use the two-way asymmetric model. That is, the principals are asked to gather information from these stakeholders to help the superintendent and the central office administrators better understand what the people are thinking about an issue so the district can plan accordingly.

Then, too, in many enlightened districts, superintendents actually engage principals in the management of the district. In other words, the principals become members of the superintendent's key publics, and he uses them to help develop the district's mission and goals and to keep it on track year in and year out. Throughout the process, the principals seek out their key publics' opinions on issues. They can do this informally, or they can do it with the help of the district's central office through questionnaires and a more formal "environmental scanning" process. The intent is to provide the superintendent with feedback from their key publics about reactions to what is going on in the district or what the stakeholders think the district should be doing that it is not. Or it might be to tip the superintendent off to changing attitudes from various sectors or neighborhoods to make him aware of something that has flown beneath his radar screen.

Before any decisions are made to go forward with the issue, superintendents will frequently bring their principals together to provide them with the rationale for the district's decision. Together, they will decide how the district should best communicate its decision to proceed. The principals are entrusted by the superintendent to be particularly insightful about how to deliver the news to their school's stakeholders. In other words, the superintendent follows their recommendations by and large for conveying the information. Active publics that may be created in opposition to the news are identified, and the superintendent and her staff can work with the principals individually or in teams to address the concerns of active publics or to counter their influence. Considerable time can be spent identifying the aware publics across the district that logically would support the issue if it were explained to them carefully. Latent publics can also be identified, and principals can then work with the district's public information officer to energize these publics in the most effective ways. Finally, the principals can be asked to identify any key stakeholders among the nonpublic—key legislators, ministers, retired board of education members, retired school employees, and city council members—if this were an issue that would ignite them. These individuals, who normally would not get involved in school business, can play pivotal roles as members of active publics if the issue resonates with them.

If the superintendent and principals are in sync, they will operate together to develop a strategic communication management approach when confronting problems with stakeholders. The first stage in the process occurs when the management team identifies a problem. They create an "issue" from the problem so that they can manage a response to it ("issue management"). At this stage, the various publics are identified, and the "hot issue" or activist publics are identified. Interpersonal communication as well as mass media should be used with activists to resolve the issue through negotiations as quickly as possible before the activist public expands.

Meanwhile, the district administrators and principals involved in the issues resolution should conduct a collaborative effort to carry out a communication management program with different stakeholders or publics. The effort should have formal objectives, such as communication, accuracy, understanding, and agreement. Generally, a central office official, probably from the communications office, should be assigned the task of evaluating the effectiveness of the effort to reduce the conflict created by the problem so that the team can better address the next conflict, because there also will be a next one.

Leaders Cover for One Another

Historically, school boards and superintendents used their principals to simply pass along directives to parents, believing that principals were closer to the clients or customers and thus better able to reach them. They were correct. The central office does its principals a disservice, however, if it continually asks them to deliver canned messages. Many of the communication problems that plague school principals, and are the subject of popular books (Ramsey, 2002), appear to stem from the fact that principals talk about things they know too little about or do not fully believe. Today's principals are going to be successful when (a) they know what they are talking about, (b) the people they are talking to know the principals have this knowledge, and (c) these people know the principal is prepared to listen to what they have to say in response.

Fortunately, most superintendents today treat their principals as members of their management teams. As such, messages crafted at the central office for distribution through the schools are vented with the principals in advance. Policies and mandates are read with the following question in mind: How will this play with the schools' stakeholders? The policy or mandate may be administered as it was originally written, but the principals may be told to let the schools' stakeholders know that the message came from the central office and any differences of opinion on it need to be resolved with the superintendent or school board, not the principals. Sometimes, that is the best the principals can hope for when dealing with an official decree from an enabling audience. It is important for principals to remember that although they are advocates for their school and for their stakeholders, they are members of the superintendent's team. The Enablers, however, should be in a position to take the heat off the principals for unpopular dictates or policies.

What about communication that goes the other way? Here is a piece of advice everyone has heard before: "Never surprise the boss." Good principals are going to work with their Partners on many things during the school year. Some of it is going to be exciting, drawing a crowd, attracting some media attention, and getting some favorable publicity to folks who depend on such things, such as elected officials.

For example, a partnership decides to have a school bazaar. It is a combination fundraiser and activity to draw together faculty, staff, students, parents, and community members. Many local merchants are involved, and some big-name state-level entertainers have already said they will participate. The local television stations have said they are going to film it, the newspapers are sending reporters and cameramen, and it appears that it could be the social highlight of the season. This is just the kind of event in which a superintendent would like to participate, as well as the chairman of the board, maybe the mayor, or members of the city council—at least the board members and city council members from the school's attendance area. Did the principal think of inviting them?

It could be worse. The principal could have forgotten to invite them and then scheduled the bazaar to take place on the weekend when the superintendent and the board members were going to be out of town at a convention. Not only would they not be present but also their absence would draw attention to the fact they were away when something important was happening. The point of this story is that communication is a two-way process.

One of the easiest ways to ensure that the school and the central office are working off the same page is to get in sync with the district's master calendar. Principals should check with their central offices before scheduling activities. If the principals can get out in front of the news, they can prepare the various publics for what is coming their way. Then, if possible, they should meet with the district's public information director, communication director, community relations chief, or whoever reports directly to the superintendent and has his back when it comes to media relations. If the district is too small to employ such a person, then the principals should meet directly with the superintendent.

The principals should explain that they are developing their own strategic communication plan and want to be sure they are in sync with the district's goals. If anybody in the district has such a district-wide plan, the communications person will. If that person does have one, he or she should be happy to share it.

When principals sit down with their communication directors to go over their districts' annual calendar, the principals should present their own school's annual plans. They should point out what they have planned that the district office might be interested in and then promise to keep the communication office informed as their planning progresses. The chances of the superintendents showing up during the year at the schools' functions increase greatly when their offices have advanced notice. Also, the chances that the superintendents will bring other dignitaries increase greatly.

Principals should not be shy about asking if it would be okay to check back during the year to find out how the districts' plans are changing, because they will. Then, they should ask if it is okay if they call occasionally if they have questions. New principals are going to need professional allies, and there is nobody better than the districts' communication chiefs. These individuals make the district look good, the superintendent look good, and the school principals look good. A smart principal takes advantage of their skills.

Principals Act as Boundary Spanners

Individuals within an organization who interact with its stakeholders and in turn gather information from them to relay to key decision makers are called boundary spanners (Aldrich & Herker, 1977, p. 217). In school districts of all sizes, elementary, middle, and secondary principals often play the role of boundary spanners for key decision makers within their central offices.

They do this because when the central office makes managerial decisions or develops policy recommendations for the school board, it will want to base them on what the district's many stakeholders believe or support. To determine this, the district can conduct a formal survey, or it can poll its principals. The principals, being "close to the customers," can generally be expected to have a good reading on their respective schools' stakeholders positions on an issue. School superintendents know from experience that their school boards will want to know what the general reaction of the stakeholders will be to any potentially controversial issue brought before it for a vote. Therefore, it behooves school superintendents to have a good reading of their districts' stakeholders, which suggests that the boundary spanners had better be good at gathering data, selecting the relevant information from what they have gathered, and then relaying it in a timely fashion to the central office.

Principals should provide the central office with information from their schools' stakeholders in a manner that fits the decision-making structure and process used by the central office. In other words, principals should not freelance. They should wait for the central office to establish the procedures for reporting the information it needs in the form and level that makes the most sense to its needs. Otherwise, the information provided is probably not going to be considered very helpful.

Nevertheless, principals who do not report seemingly irrelevant information from stakeholders may be doing their districts a tremendous disservice. Nowhere is that point made better than in graduate courses in public relations in which students are exposed to a case study involving Nestlé's ill-fated marketing decision in the 1970s to convince mothers in aspiring Third World families to switch from breast-feeding to more "modern" bottle feeding. What was ignored was the unintended consequence of mixing inadequate quantities of the infant formula with contaminated water in many of the Third World nations where Nestlé marketed its product. Many infants died from malnutrition and disease. Consequently, activists worldwide organized international boycotts of Nestlé's products to protest the company. Is it possible that everyone in the company was so focused on marketing the product that nobody felt empowered to ask how the consumer was likely to actually use it on a daily basis?

Consider the hand wringing that goes on in a school district after a student shooting. The principal, teachers, guidance counselors, security personnel, and parents start to assemble what they knew about the youngster who pulled the trigger, and they realize that had they done this exercise in advance they may have been able to prevent the tragedy that unfolded.

In the best circumstances, the superintendent will create a formal mechanism for principals to report regularly about stakeholders' attitudes and opinions about school district issues and problems. If superintendents do not establish such a mechanism, principals need to find a direct avenue to superintendents or one of their key staff members so that they can be tipped off when an aware public of stakeholders is forming that has the potential to become a hostile active public unless its issues are addressed promptly.

Principals Should Be Consultants to the Superintendent

Just as some superintendents will ask their principals to provide them with regular updates of their stakeholders' opinions and attitudes toward district issues and problems, some superintendents will also consult with their principals when it is time to deal with these matters. Of course, not all decisions are of equal importance. In fact, most of the decisions made by central offices are probably the "operational" kind. Principals hardly need to be consulted about these decisions and would be upset to think they had to be consulted.

Some issues and problems, however, generate a class of decisions that are described as "strategic decisions" (Jemison, 1984, p. 132). These profoundly affect the future success and destiny of the district's mission and as such should involve the school principals as key leaders of the individual stakeholder networks.

Superintendents find themselves making decisions about "complex" or "wicked" problems that have the following characteristics (White & Dozier, 1992, p. 98):

- Inadequate information is available to decision makers.
- Multiple and conflicting objectives are involved.
- Several decision makers are involved.
- The problem environment is dynamic and turbulent.
- Several such problems are linked together.
- Resolution may involve costly, irreversible commitments.

These are decisions that principals do not necessarily want to make; they undoubtedly want to express an opinion from their stakeholders' viewpoint, however.

Normally, when a school district has a wicked problem, it tries to forge a resolution that will satisfy as many people as possible. For example, in 2004 a northern Virginia suburban school district school superintendent and one of her board members were pulled over by a city policeman several hours after a school meeting had ended. The superintendent was cited for driving under the influence of alcohol. She later went to court, pleaded guilty, was fined, and had her driver's license revoked. Her problems had only begun, however. A vocal movement began in the community, led by the vice chair of the school board, to have her fired. The school board, who had already agreed to extend her contract, was unwilling to fire her over this driving infraction. The active public in opposition to her, however, was well organized, had generated extensive media coverage, and was not going to go away.

The well-respected principal of the city's only public high school was consulted by the board members. They wanted a reading of his key publics. The board members were concerned that the superintendent's behavior might compromise a major effort at the high school to crack down on teenage drinking. The board members knew the principal's reading of his publics' views (including his students and their parents and teachers) would be instrumental in how they would eventually resolve the matter with the superintendent.

Finally, with all the data it could obtain, the board met in a private session with the superintendent and told her what it would require of her to retain her job while satisfying her critics. Then, the board and the superintendent went into a public session and announced that she had been ordered into an alcohol treatment program and that 1 year of her contract had been rescinded. The board also said that she retained her job, and that she was entitled to receive an automatic pay raise for the successful year she just completed. Neither party was totally satisfied, but both accepted the compromise and agreed to move on "for the benefit of the district." There was little question that the principal's reading of the situation swayed the board's thinking and satisfied the community's need for closure.

Being a Boundary Spanner Can Have a Downside

Principals may or may not find themselves part of the decision-making process in the central office. It depends on the management style of the superintendent and the school board, of course. Increasingly, however, superintendents determined to improve the academic achievement of their districts' schools are investing heavily to build the teamwork necessary to ensure that this happens. This generally begins with the development of a close working relationship between the superintendent and the principals. A good sign, as indicated previously, is when superintendents make a point of asking their principals to provide them with regular and ongoing "scanning" of their stakeholders so that the superintendents know their views on issues and problems affecting the districts.

Principals may logically expect superintendents to tip them off to issues and problems before they go public. This does not always happen, however. It is the paradox of being a boundary spanner. The central office may well have a concern that principals with such ready access to their schools' stakeholders should not have full access to information about the district's problems for fear they will share them prematurely or inappropriately. Aldrich and Herker (1977) noted that "boundary-spanning individuals, although exerting some influence within the organization because of their external information, may be denied greater influence because their loyalty is suspect" (p. 220).

As a consequence, principals walk a fine line. On the one hand, they must be school leaders willing to use the two-way symmetric communication model in their own schools to obtain information so that they can challenge the central office when it prepares to make management decisions based on a faulty reading of the district's stakeholders. On the other hand, these principals face possible exclusion from district decision making because their closeness to the stakeholders makes the central office suspicious of their motives.

In the long term, of course, the principals who help the district make better decisions are doing the right thing. In the short term, the principals must maintain the trust of the central office even while they pass along what may be stakeholder information or feedback that it would just as soon not hear.

Principals Need to Read and Understand Data

School leaders will occasionally find themselves confronted by hostile active publics bearing data. The data will support their cause or tear down the position advocated by the district. Generally, with a room full of people watching, principals will be asked to read an article and often be asked to confirm the group's opinion about what it says. Armed with this new bit of data, the hostile active public will want to make changes on the spot. What is a principal to do?

Principals can begin by setting examples that show how their stakeholders should use data. If principals never come to a meeting with copies of a single journal article to bolster their argument for change, they will be off to a good start. Principals should be willing to provide stakeholders with multiple perspectives on an issue. Not everybody will see the issue exactly the same way. Principals are kidding themselves if they think they are helping their case by holding back arguments against their positions. These eventually surface and will show up at meetings as "gotcha" items.

A principal preparing to make a case for something should prepare for it much like an editorial page editor prepares to write an editorial advocating a point of view. The principal who wishes to advocate a position should start by making the case for why something needs to be done. Then he should introduce the argument for the alternatives and explain briefly why he has rejected each of them. Next, he slowly, logically, needs to make the case for his solution and conclude with a strong closing argument for action steps to be taken. If the stakeholders know this is how their principal conducts business, they are less likely to demand immediate action based on the reading of one new piece of information.

Principals can also train their closest stakeholders—Partners and Enablers—to "read data, not rhetoric." Consider the example shown in Box 7.1.

Box 7.1   Independent Study Shows Teach for America Impact on Student Achievement

---

Mathematica Policy Research, Inc., a leading research firm, released an independent study that demonstrates Teach for America's effectiveness in the classroom. The study compared the academic gains of students taught by Teach for America corps members with the gains of similar students taught by other teachers, both new and veteran, in the same schools and grades.

The study finds that Teach for America corps members:

- Make 10% more progress in a year in math than is typically expected, while slightly exceeding the normal expectation for progress in reading;

- Attain great gains in math and the same gains in reading compared to the other teachers in the study, even as compared only to certified teachers and to veteran teachers; and
- Are working toward our mission in the highest-need classrooms in the country.

The study's findings should move us beyond the debate about whether Teach for America is a good thing. The report is clear: "Even though Teach for America teachers generally lack formal teacher training beyond that provided by Teach for America, they produce similar scores as the other teachers in their schools—not just other novice teachers, but also veteran and certified teachers" (Teach for America Web site).

The issue here, of course, is the long-standing debate in education circles regarding whether young, enthusiastic, bright people without traditional teacher training can do as well in the classroom as teachers who have taken teacher education courses. The Mathematica study suggests the answer is yes.

The Teach for America (TFA) Web site provided a link to the Mathematica Policy Research Web site, where it prominently displayed a press release of the study. TFA's headline said, "Teach for America teachers outperform novice and veteran colleagues in math; achieve the same results in reading as their peers, national study reveals." The vice president and principal investigator for Mathematica was quoted as saying, "TFA teachers not only had more success than other novice teachers, but they had more success than teachers with an average of 6 years of experience in the classroom."

The press release states that the Mathematica study was based on a large national sample of 100 classrooms in 17 schools in six geographical high-poverty areas: Baltimore, Chicago, Houston, and Los Angeles (the City of Compton), New Orleans, and the Mississippi Delta. The Mathematica researchers randomly assigned students in the study to either TFA teachers or control group teachers. Student performance was then measured at the beginning and end of the same academic year (Mathematica Web site). Although TFA certainly put a positive spin on the study's findings, the 64-page-long study was available at the time on Mathematica's Web site for anyone to review.

This is an excellent example of why principals need to "read the data, not just the rhetoric." Although at first blush the study seems to bolster the argument that hiring TFA members makes good sense, a careful reading of the data may give thoughtful principals some pause.

One of the country's better education reporters, Jay Mathews of the *Washington Post*, cut through the rhetoric in an article soon after the Mathematica report went public. He pointed out that although the TFA teachers outperformed the non-TFA teachers in the control group, they did not raise student achievement to intended levels. Yes, their students' math scores increased by 3 percentile points. What the press release did not say, and the full report makes clear, is that the gain was similar to Mathews's batting average in the Old Folks League going from .067 to .073. In the fall, the TFA students scored on average at the 14th percentile in math. By spring, they scored at the 15th percentile. Mathews (2004) wrote,

> This was better than the control group students, who were at the 15th percentile in the fall and still there in the spring, but I don't think anyone would regard this as an impressive gain. In reading, the numbers are similarly depressing: The TFA students went from the 14th to the 15th percentile and the control group students went from the 13th to the 14th percentile.

Linda Darling-Hammond (Stanford University education professor) said (as quoted in Mathews, 2004),

> The study documents the failure of the public policy approach these districts and states have adopted for staffing their high-minority schools—an approach in which slightly trained TFA teachers look better than other poorly trained hires but none of them actually improve student achievement to any great degree.

Principals Need to Be on Guard

The point of this exercise is to demonstrate that principals need to be on guard against friend and foe alike who would promote their agenda through the use of a little data and a lot of rhetoric. Principals should work with their Partners to get used to debunking the myths and exposing the faulty thinking that permeates all levels of educational discussions today. Principals who do not know what studies actually say, and rely instead on press releases and news reports, are vulnerable to half-truths and spun data. Worse yet, they contribute to the preservation of education myths that have a habit of living long after good data should have put a stake in them and buried them for good.

No principal, of course, can possibly keep up with all the research. Nor can principals expect to remain abreast of every point-counterpoint discussion going on in academic circles about the relative merits of one approach to reading versus another approach, for example. Principals can stay on top of the major educational issues of the day, however, by reading such publications as *Education Week* and those published by their state and national principal associations.

Principals may also wish to invest some time and effort into reading the work of Gerald W. Bracey. In a monthly column in *Phi Delta Kappan*, he attempts to sort out what educational research says to practitioners. Equally important, his occasional books are helpful guides to school leaders who frequently find themselves confused when trying to determine who and what to believe with regard to sorting out myths from realities in education.

For example, Bracey's book, *Bail Me Out: Handling Difficult Data and Tough Questions About Public Schools* (2000), provides "principles of data interpretation or how to keep from getting statistically snookered" and a whole section on "handling tough questions." Principals will appreciate the latter. It helps them frame answers to such questions as "Why are test scores falling?" "Why are we throwing money at schools?" and "Why are teachers and administrators not held accountable?"

Bracey (2000) wants principals to know that taking on the defense of public schools is no easy chore. He believes, as he has often written,

> There is a neurotic need to believe the worst about our schools. Schools are our most personally public institution. You can blame government for problems. But "government" is somehow remote. Schools are concrete, and their representatives walk among the local citizens every day. (p. 199)

Bracey (2000) goes on to say,

> Even though pundits have of late been pronouncing another recession as "inevitable" but predictable, when it does happen, some will try to lay the blame at the schoolhouse door. I can only urge persistence. When people say you're being defensive, say that these are the facts and they are not being selected or spun. Invite your accuser to offer other facts. When people say you're just acting in your own self-interest, admit

that, yes, it is in my self-interest to produce the facts. Invite your accuser to offer other facts. (p. 199)

Bracey reminds his readers that most people get their news about the nation's schools from the media, but when asked about where they get information about local schools, they say from local sources. One of the reasons people tend to be more positive about local schools than schools in general is because the information they have about local schools comes from reliable and trustworthy sources. The message for local principals is that they are frequently the sources of this local information. Thus, they need to work to keep a steady stream of news about the local schools flowing to the stakeholders so that it can be passed on from them to the larger community.

There is no dearth of problems in education, and the general public is certainly aware of most of them. Principals need to be prepared to talk honestly about these challenges and what it will take to overcome them. At the same time, principals need to remind their stakeholders about the many educational accomplishments occurring every day at the local schools. The principals will realize that there is a receptive audience out there for that message, and it consists of the schools' Partners, beginning with its parents, community members, and faculty. When a principal has them "on message," managing communications with the broader group of stakeholders is easy.

Bracey is not the only one worrying about this issue. Willis Hawley, the emeritus dean of the college of education at the University of Maryland, College Park, talks about how it is almost always problematic to use "the latest" study on a topic or any particular study or, for that matter, to rely on a single expert (W. Hawley, personal communication, April 29, 2005). Hawley, a first-rate scholar, suggests that school leaders involve teachers in identifying the best thinking on a topic. He says that a teacher study group is often productive because it builds expertise within the school that can be called on when issues arise. Hawley also says that the search costs for knowledge about best practice can be reduced significantly by relying on syntheses of research that have the following characteristics:

1. A panel of nationally recognized experts is involved.

2. The criteria for selecting research to be reviewed is clear.

3. The synthesis is peer reviewed.

4. The source of support (e.g., funding) for the research review does not have a say in the conclusions reached.

Among the sources that fit these characteristics are the National Research Council (for a list of studies, see www.nap.edu) and the What Works Clearinghouse (www.w-w-c.org), which was established in 2002. Syntheses of research found in two journals of the American Educational Research Association, *Review of Educational Research* and *Review of Research in Education*, are not the work of panels but otherwise meet the previous best-practice characteristics listed previously.

Summary

In this chapter, principals were reminded that they need to work with their central offices to ensure that they communicate with one another so that activities being planned at the district and the school do not surprise either the principals or the central offices. The chapter also explained how principals serve as boundary spanners in that they interact with the district's stakeholders and frequently gather, select, and relay information about their stakeholders' attitudes and opinions regarding issues and problems. Armed with this information, the principals are able to inform central office decision makers on a regular basis. This information then becomes part of the process used for decision making by the superintendent or the school board or both.

In some cases, superintendents are apt to involve principals in the decision-making process. There is a tendency among some central office staff, however, to exclude them from management meetings for the simple reason that they are viewed as too close to their own stakeholders to be fully trusted. Principals must learn to walk a fine line between maintaining the trust of the central office and being willing to provide it with disturbing and unwelcome input from their stakeholders' perspectives.

Finally, principals need to read data, not rhetoric. By the same token, they need to defend against others who do not.

8

Using Technology in Communication

Technology has made communication nearly instantaneous. From e-mail to instant messaging, Web sites, and blogs, technology has both enhanced communication and added an additional burden of expected and immediate two-way communication. Every principal should be using technology to the fullest for effective communication but also should be aware of the potential pitfalls. Principals should not let the school Web site, e-mail, and cell phones become communication crutches, and the traditional communication techniques discussed in this chapter should not be abandoned.

The "old-fashioned" communication techniques are not being replaced by technology. Technology simply adds different tools that make communication faster, easier, and more frequent. As Epstein (2004, p. 3) noted, "Technology is a critical and increasingly complex tool for implementing effective partnership programs," and principals need to communicate using both "high-tech" and "low-tech" strategies. On the one hand, a principal may believe that communication technology makes the job more difficult—more mediums, more information, more demand. On the other hand, a more positive outlook would be to embrace the thought that technology gives principals the ability to communicate more frequently and more proactively.

Building a School Web Site

The Internet is continuing to evolve as the first resource people check for information. From directions and maps to shopping, researching new products, checking the news, and chatting with friends and family, increasingly more parents, students, and community members rely on the Internet for information. That sought out information includes comparative school data and test scores on district and state sites as well as sites such as www.schoolmatters.com and www .just4 kids.com. In fact, 63% of the population is online, according to Mediamark Research (www.mediamark.com). This statistic is probably fairly conservative. Those that do use the Internet are typically younger and more educated. Therefore, a principal's key audiences are more than likely e-mail and Web site users. Even in more urban, lower-income communities, e-mail and Web site access continues to increase. Almost all students are online. The U.S. Census Bureau reported in 2003 that four of five school-aged children are regularly online, including elementary-aged children, and "families with children under 18 are more likely to have computers than families without children" (www.ntia.doc.gov). It is no wonder that "google" is now used as a verb in everyday conversation (Box 8.1).

Box 8.1   Just Google

Google yourself, google the school, google the district. Take a close look at the Web site hits and hit the news tab at the top to see what "news" items are found. Do not just do it once; make it part of your regular schedule. Sign up for the Google News Alerts with the key words including your name, the school's name, and the district, as well as any nearby principals, schools, districts, and any pertinent issues. Whenever any of these appear in the media, you will know and be able to stay well informed. Parents and key audiences have you on their "Google" list already.

In addition, bookmark sites such as www.schoolmatters .org and www.just4kids.org to keep abreast on the news and rankings. Parents and other active publics are turning to sites such as these to find out how their child's school compares to others close to home and throughout the country.

The school's Web site is a key communication tool. The more information on the site, the better. Aware and active publics are seeking information and, more than likely, would prefer the convenience and efficiency of gathering the data online rather than making a phone call or setting up a meeting. Eventually, parents and other key publics will start checking the Web site first before calling the office with questions, saving everyone time. Today, schools cannot afford not to be on the Web. Parents, teachers, students, and the community at large expect to log onto a Web site and find anything they are looking for with just a few clicks. The Web site should become a principal's best tool for communicating with the largest number of key stakeholders. Keeping the facts straight, the rumor mill at bay, and important information at the fingertips of the stakeholders are just a few of the benefits of a good Web site.

It is important to realize that the Web site is going to be used by many different stakeholders. These multiple audiences should be taken into consideration when developing a Web site. For elementary school principals, the primary users of the Web site will be parents, grandparents, and partners. For middle and high school principals, it is likely that both students and adults will be accessing the site for information.

Whether the school already has a Web site or still needs to develop one, principals need to work with the district office. Principals should talk to the district information technology (IT) department to determine what is possible and what resources are available. For some districts, principals may have access to a staff of savvy Web developers and technology gurus. In others, there may be only one overworked IT professional. Fortunately, the Web site technology that is now readily available makes updating and building a Web site fairly straightforward. Easy maintenance is key because an effective Web site is not static but, rather, regularly updated with timely information. There is much technology happening behind Web sites, such as meta-tags and tracking software, and having a knowledgeable IT professional on a principal's side is extremely helpful. The best scenario for any Web site would be to have a dedicated Web master. Although that is unlikely, principals should look to the communications team to develop a small group that is dedicated to providing an excellent Web site for the school.

Many districts provide Web site guidelines that can often be accessed online. For example, the Corpus Christi Independent School District has a comprehensive Web site development handbook online (corpuschristiisd.org) that is a good reference if a district is without guidelines. Principals need to understand their audience and design the site with their needs in mind, however, and that may differ from the district's guidelines of what should be on the site.

For example, many schools have extremely long and complicated URLs (or Web site addresses) based on the district's Web site. Ensuring that the Web address is simple and easy to remember is the start to an effective Web site. Principals should make it very easy for everyone to access the site without much thought or effort.

The basics of a good Web site include navigation, timeliness, design, and, most important, content. Principals should examine what other schools are doing (Box 8.2), but the review should not be limited to elementary, middle, and high school Web sites. Principals should spend time on the district's Web site as well as surrounding districts' sites. Other sites to visit include those of community colleges and universities, area chamber of commerce and other businesses, and children's sport leagues.

Box 8.2   The Best on the Web

Not sure where to start? Before you start uploading pages to your site, take time to plan and examine what other schools are doing online. Surf the sites below and "Google" schools throughout the country to see the many ways principals are using Web sites and gather hints on content and resources from district sites. Take the best from these Web sites to develop the very best school Web site.

Montgomery County, Maryland: www.mcps.k12.md.us; Montgomery Blair High School, http://www.mbhs.edu

Prince William County, Virginia: www.pwcs.edu; Woodbridge Senior High School, www.wshsvikings.org

Plano, Texas: www.pisd.edu; Wyatt Elementary School, k-12.pisd.edu/schools/wyatt/index.htm

Vancouver, Washington: www.vansd.org; Skyview High School, www.skyview.vansd.org

> Greenville County, South Carolina: www.greenville.k12
> .sc.us/index.asp; Taylor Elementary School, www.greenville
> .k12.sc.us/taylorse
>
> Fairfax County, Virginia: www.fcps.k12.va.us; Lake Braddock
> Secondary School, www.fcps.edu/LakeBraddockSS
>
> Cherry Creek, Colorado: www.ccsd.k12.co.us/index.htm;
> Prairie Middle School, www.pms.ccsd.k12.co.us
>
> Poway Unified School District, Poway, California: powayusd
> .sdcoe.k12.ca.us; Mesa Verde Middle School, www.pusd.info/
> pusdmvms/default.htm
>
> Blue Valley, Kansas: www.bluevalleyk12.org; Blue Valley
> Northwest High, www.bv229.k12.ks.us/BVNW

Navigation

Principals need to make it easy for users to find information quickly. Layers upon layers of links and subpages are frustrating. Clear navigational links are essential. School Web sites need to be user-friendly to a number of different groups, particularly parents and students who will be accessing the site for very different reasons. Therefore, there should be a balance of school spirit and fun pages for the children and a professional, informational image for the parents. It may also be beneficial to create two main subpages—one for students and one for parents and other Partners.

Not many school Web sites include site maps and a search function. These two elements are now considered basics on any site. Principals who include them on the Web site are making communication easier for key audiences.

Design

Keep it simple. Lots of colors, background designs, moving items, and photos are distracting and slow the loading time for the Web page. Many stakeholders may be using dial-up connections. The school site should be information driven with an easy-to-read font and a unified image across all pages. Of course, principals and communication teams can have some fun by using school colors, playing on the school's mascot and theme, and making the site attractive to both parents and students.

Online, users' eyes tend to move toward the upper left corner of a Web site. This is where Web surfers typically find corporate logos. Navigational bars tend to be across the top and down the left side. Because of screen sizes and monitor resolutions, using this area for key elements is important, and keeping content uncluttered without frames and the need for too much scrolling is essential to eliminating user frustration.

Content

Content is king on the Web and key for a school Web site. Obviously, content will vary from elementary to middle and high schools. See Box 8.3 for items that could be on a school's Web site. This is not intended to be a comprehensive list but, rather, a list to get a principal and the communications team thinking about what needs to be online. Anything that is sent home on paper should be posted on the Web site at a minimum. Principals should refer to the Web site on all written communication. (For more details on this matter, visit www.ourschool.edu.) Messages to latent audiences should encourage them to visit the Web site. In fact, every piece of communication from the school—from the principal's business card to stationery and score boards at the stadium—should display the Web address prominently.

When developing the copy, whether it be a monthly note from the principal or information on testing, the content should be concise and without "educationese." Principals should speak to the stakeholders in a clear and straightforward manner. Everyone on the communications team should learn to spell-check and review everything before it is uploaded. Grammatical and spelling errors on the Web site are as unforgivable as those in letters or memos.

Principals should make documents available in both "pdf" and "html" formats. Currently, many schools do not offer this option; many users prefer one version or the other, however. Instead of offering one or the other, school Web sites should offer both, and one of those options should be printer friendly. Many parents and users will decide to print out handbooks, the phone/e-mail list, or lunch menus. Also, the principal will probably want them to print some of the items, such as an emergency guide.

The site should be updated frequently with current information. With a Web team in place, updating the site should be a regular task—part of a daily routine. Parents searching for back-to-school supply lists will be up in arms if "Have a great summer!" is still posted during the middle of August. During the school year, it is even more important that the Web site is full of current information.

Principals should also ask for input from teachers, the PTA, and Partners. Do they have items to contribute? What would they most like to see on the Web site? The principal should welcome input and content from many sources but keep updates to the core Web team. The principal still needs to be able to manage the Web site, and for both good and bad, technology has made it so easy for even some of the most non-tech savvy to do so. Therefore, updating the site should be left to the core team, or it soon could get out of control.

The Web site can also be a key tool before and during a crisis. For example, Prince William County, Virginia, has a quick reference audience guide for dealing with crises as well as a crisis emergency preparedness brochure at www.pwcs.edu. To be an effective communicator, principals need to take a close look at the school's stakeholders and get to know them. Is the school located in a multilingual community? If so, publishing the site in another language is another way to encourage involvement and make the task of reviewing information much easier, especially for parents. Many parents whose second language is English are mired in the latent public, and language is a key communication barrier. By reaching out to them using their native language, a principal makes the first step to encourage this group to move from latent to the aware, and potentially to a friend with time.

Even if the task of translating the entire site into a different language seems daunting, key sections, such as "A Message From the Principal," "Emergency Preparedness Guide," and "Discipline Policies," should be made available in multiple languages so that everyone in the community can access and understand the information. For example, San Diego City Public School's superintendent publishes his letter to parents in both English and Spanish (www .sdcs.k12.ca.us). Miami-Dade County Public Schools publishes its Web site in English, Spanish, and Creole (www.dadeschools). Montgomery County Public Schools is translating its parent's guide into Spanish, Chinese, Korean, French, and Vietnamese.

Box 8.3   Web Site Content Menu

- About our school
  - School fact sheet—history, mission, mascot and colors, etc.
  - Message from the principal
  - Annual report
  - Map and directions
  - Safety, behavior, and discipline policies
  - School handbook
  - Emergency preparedness manual
  - Enrollment forms and information
  - School hours
  - Bus information

- School report card
  - NCLB statistics and results

- News and events
  - School calendar
  - Photos and wrap-ups from past events
  - Newsletter
  - News releases student newspaper
  - Submit announcement function

- Lunch menus
- Individual classroom pages
  - Field trip details
  - Supply lists

- Department pages
  - Guidance counselor page
  - Including college/career links
  - Library/media center page
  - Including helpful research links
  - Homework help
  - Nurse's page
  - Immunization information
  - Health alert

- Student leadership page
- Extracurricular activities—sports and clubs
- Student accomplishments (awards, artwork, poems, etc.)

- Resources
  - Feeder/sending schools (i.e., for elementary, links to middle and high school)
  - Resources for parents and caregivers
  - District Web site
  - Teacher resources
  - Handbook
  - Human resources link
  - Involvement/PTA page
  - Volunteer guide
- Community links
  - County Web site
  - Day care facilities
  - Traffic cams
  - Weather
- Alumni news
- Surveys
- Contact us
  - Feedback/comments e-mail link
  - Staff phone and e-mail list
- Site map
- Search function

Remember, anything that the principal would send home on paper should be posted on the Web site.

Frequently, much of the information that should be on the school's Web site may already be on the district's site. Rather than duplicate, the school site should include links to the district's Web site or any other resources with permission. Although links are extremely helpful, principals and communication teams need to develop a system to fix broken links quickly. When linking to another site, school sites should force a new window to open. This small addition will keep visitors at the school site.

So far, this discussion has only touched on how the Web site can be an effective and efficient one-way communication tool. The beauty of the Internet, however, is its ability for quick and easy two-way communication. The Web site should be a forum for visitors to communicate easily with the principal or anyone in the school. "Contact

Us" is one of the key elements that is needed on the Web site. Anyone who accesses the site needs to be able to submit a comment form, send an e-mail, and look up the snail mail address and telephone number. It may seem that by posting the principal's e-mail address, the flow of e-mails will be overwhelming. Principals do not need to go it alone. Instead, all teacher and staff member's e-mail addresses should be prominently posted and easy to find so that users can contact them directly if needed. For example, Wilde Lake High School in Howard County, MD, includes short biographies and hot-linked e-mail addresses of its teachers (www.wildelake.com).

The site should encourage feedback that includes a feedback form for comments or an area where parents can sign up to have a monthly newsletter e-mailed to them. Other additions to encourage two-way communication include the following:

- A monthly "what do you think" question
- A volunteer registration form
- A survey on a new initiative

A Web site is more than just a one-way communication tool. It provides an opportunity for stakeholders to easily communicate with the principal and the school.

The Web site has the potential to be so much more. College degrees can now be obtained through online classes. Live discussion groups and book clubs meet online. Video conferencing online has brought Web seminars and meetings to life. According to the Pew Internet & American Life Project, more than 53 million Americans communicate via instant messaging, and it is a favorite with teenagers. These are examples of just some of the next generation of technology that will eventually be a part of the school's communications and teaching program. These are the tools that are making the Internet a key two-way communication tool.

Some schools are experimenting with forums, chat rooms, and blogs for parents, students, and community members. This can be a great platform for discussion, but if not carefully monitored, it can quickly get out of hand. Many teachers have noted that posting discussion questions and assignments has been a tremendous help in managing a student's education. The list of what can be placed on a Web site, and the services that can be provided, continues to grow, including password-protected areas to post grades and performance updates and online surveys for parents and the community. Although this does not directly affect a principal's personal communication efforts, these are issues that should be monitored.

In conjunction with the district, principals can include options for parents to receive newsletters and other urgent information via e-mail. For example, in Fairfax County, Virginia, messages are sent by e-mail through the "Keep in Touch" system (www.fcps.medianext .com). There are also third-party technology providers such as School's Out (www.schools-out.com), which offers services to e-mail parents on school closures due to weather incidents.

Unfortunately, as with all types of communication, Web sites have potential legal pitfalls. The use of student, volunteer, and staff images, as well as examples of excellent student work, requires release forms. In addition to a host of general intellectual property issues from copyright to trademark, there is a long list of regulations that must be considered, including the Children's Online Privacy Protection Act (COPPA), Children's Internet Protection Act (CIPA), Family Educational Rights and Privacy Act (FERPA), the Digital Millennium Copyright Act of 1998, and Americans with Disabilities Act (ADA). It is hoped that the district's counsel is on top of these issues and should be able to provide guidance. It is important for principals to be familiar with these rules and regulations, however, because they are ultimately responsible for their school's Web site.

For example, accessibility is a key issue. According to www .webstyleguide.com,

> For many organizations, providing equal access to Web pages is institutional policy, if not a federal mandate. It is critical, therefore, that you validate your designs and page templates and the content of your site throughout the development process to ensure that your pages are accessible to all users. To check the accessibility of your pages you can use a tool like Bobby (www.cast.org/bobby). Bobby is a free service provided by the Center for Applied Special Technology. After you supply the URL (Uniform Resource Locator) of your page, Bobby checks the page against the Web Accessibility Initiative guidelines and flags potential barriers for users with disabilities. Bobby also recommends changes that will improve the accessibility of your pages. Check your designs at every development milestone to avoid time-consuming and potentially costly revamping efforts.

Just because a principal has just built the best school Web site possible does not mean that visitors will flock there. When the new or updated site launches, it should be treated the same as an announcement of a new initiative or other good news. As noted previously, the Web site address needs to be on every form of communication that comes from the school, from a link in e-mail signatures to all forms of written communication including the school's letterhead, right next to the phone number and address. Principals can find creative ways of communicating their Web site address, such as incorporating it as part of their "on-hold" messages for their phone and voice-mail. The Web site team should also search for reciprocal linking opportunities. Chambers of commerce, real estate agents, and even local media Web sites are probably willing to add a link to the school's Web site for free. In addition to keeping the content current, Web site statistics should be reviewed monthly. Web site traffic reports can provide a wealth of information. For example, these reports will describe which pages are most popular and how visitors navigate through the site. Principals may find that everyone seems to be looking at the lunch menu, but very few are looking at the emergency preparedness guide. Overall, these reports will give the principal a good idea which pages are most frequently viewed and what areas need to be publicized in other mediums or what pages and navigation tools need improvement. For example, Montgomery County's Public Schools (MD) district's site had a greater than 80% increase in site traffic from 2003 to 2004. Thus, they decided to asked visitors to fill out a survey with questions on topics ranging from ease of navigation to Internet access speed. MCPS won the National School Public Relations Association's Gold Medallion award in 2004 for its redesigned site. That does not mean that they are sitting on their laurels, however. Continuous improvement is obviously part of the system's communication plan.

Making Effective Use of E-Mail

Just as a well-constructed Web site is now expected, the use of e-mail is even more so. This is especially true with busy parents who are actively involved in their children's education but also are professionals who access e-mail from work, home, and even on the road and would rather use e-mail than face-to-face meetings, or even the phone, to communicate. Other stakeholders, such as reporters, editors, and community leaders, frequently prefer e-mail to any other type of communication. Principals need to ask how these other stakeholders prefer to be contacted, particularly Partners. Even if the response is e-mail, that does not mean all other forms of communication should be abandoned but, rather, they should be used frequently.

Principals need to encourage everyone in the school to use e-mail effectively and efficiently, including checking and responding to e-mail every day (Box 8.4). Unfortunately, that may not always be reality, but communicating via e-mail is becoming a standard practice in schools. E-mail can be a very useful tool for everyone from teachers to the school nurse. For example, a teacher may choose to set up report card conferences via e-mail rather than send home paper slips. The school nurse may be having a difficult time getting in touch with a busy executive with a sick child. In addition to the home, work, and cell phone numbers, a quick e-mail may actually reach a mother faster.

Therefore, how do a principal and the communication team develop a database that is comprehensive? The questions should be posed everywhere and at every opportunity. There should be a link on the Web site for parents to sign up for e-mail alerts and updates. Registration and information forms should have a line for parents' e-mail addresses. It may take some time to build a good database, but as soon as the school starts sending out e-mails, word will quickly spread that information is coming via e-mail and that people should visit the Web site to sign up.

Box 8.4   E-Mail Tips

Remember the medium.

- Write e-mails with the understanding that they could easily be forwarded to hundreds of people. There is no such thing as a private e-mail.
- Be careful with attachments. If you need to attach a document, make sure the file is not too large.
- With sensitive subjects, long and involved e-mails are not as appropriate as phone calls if the principal believes an e-mail response would not be sufficient and a conversation would be more appropriate.
- Develop an e-mail filing system, probably best organized by topic. File e-mails from parents, teachers, and other key publics.
- Hit "reply" instead of starting a new e-mail so the original message is included at the bottom, and write the response at the top. Avoid answering questions within the body of the original e-mail. Embedded notes are frequently missed.

(Continued)

Box 8.4 (Continued)

Be responsive.

- Answer e-mails as you would voice mails in a timely manner—within 24 hours.
- Set aside two or three times a day to respond to e-mails so they do not pile up and become overwhelming. Do not feel that each one needs to be answered as it arrives in your in-box. If you do, you will never leave your desk.
- Use the automatic "out of office reply" if you will not be able to check your e-mail for any period of time longer than 24 hours and include in your response when you will be back in the office.
- Consider using a Blackberry or other portable e-mail device.
- Be proactive. Use e-mail to inform and update key audiences, particularly those that you know prefer to receive e-mails rather than phone calls.
- Watch out for "flames" or venting and inflammatory e-mails. Respond to these only when necessary, and do not "flame" back. Angry e-mails do not require an equally angry response.

Keep it business.

- Spell check. Reread and edit before hitting the "send" button.
- Write active subject lines. Make sure the recipient will have an idea of the content of the e-mail from the subject line. Also, keep the body of the e-mail concise.
- Unfortunately, facial expressions and tone that are appropriate in face-to-face conversations do not convey well in e-mails. Keep your e-mails straightforward and professional by avoiding sarcasm and smiley faces (emoticons).
- Use the automatic signature so your contact information is always included at the end of your e-mails, including a disclaimer.
- Keep your professional and personal e-mail separate. Use different accounts—one for stakeholders and one for friends and family.
- By the way (BTW), avoid common chat room abbreviations. The recipient of your e-mail may not know the abbreviations and will not LOL (laugh out loud).

Technology Issues
Principals Should Be Aware Of

As noted previously, along with expanded communication tools come additional problems. No longer is the main concern whether the copier has enough toner; with e-mail comes the worry of spam. With an increased networked school system come the fear of worms and viruses as well as security issues and hackers. These are more reasons why a principal will need to develop strong relationships with the district's IT staff. Principals should utilize the district resources and also spend the time to educate themselves. *Legal Issues & Education Technology: A School Leader's Guide*, a National School Boards Association Council of School Attorneys' publication, describes strategies to prevent legal dilemmas and includes topics such as legal requirements for accessible Web sites; student and staff privacy rights; COPPA, CIPA, FERPA, and ADA compliance issues and updates; copyrights; and acceptable use policies.

The following are several simple guidelines, but they are not intended to be legal advice. Principals should remember that electronic communication, whether through e-mail or on the school Web site, can initiate the same legal action that other methods of communication can and should look to the district office for more comprehensive guidance.

- Do not delete e-mails.
- Do not post photos of students, teachers, or volunteers on the Web site without written approval.
- Remember that e-mails are not private.
- Save your personal surfing and Web shopping for your home computer.
- Include a disclaimer on your e-mail signature.
- Adopt and post a privacy policy if you are gathering e-mails for electronic newsletter distribution and so on, or provide a link to the district's privacy statement. (See www.mcps.k12.md.us)
- Ask for permission to link to any outside resources and Web sites.
- Keep a backup of the Web site.

Using Cell Phones and More Telephones

According to the Cellular Telecommunications & Internet Association (CTIA; www.ctia.org), there are more than 166 million wireless telecommunication users in the United States, and this number increases every day. In fact, CTIA monitors the number of cell phone users hourly. Today, it is unusual to find many people without a cell phone. Many parents and members of key publics, as well as many students, probably have a cell phone in their pocket.

Typically, principals have managed phone conversations and messages from their desks. Time at a desk, however, is time that the principal is not visible to others—an important factor in effective communication. When visible, walking around the school, visiting community members, or meeting outside the school, the principal is not readily available for phone calls. Today, especially in the corporate world, parents, community leaders, reporters, and politicians expect instant and easy access via cell phone.

How will carrying a cell phone benefit a principal's communication with others? First, principals need to get comfortable using it and using it frequently. Cell phone conversations do not need to be lengthy or in-depth. The more serious issues can be saved for the landline in the office away from other distractions, dropped calls, and the inevitable "can you hear me now?" Cell phones are a great way to keep in touch—even if a principal is just leaving voice mail messages to keep key publics up-to-date.

Consider, for example, Principal Charles Sposato of the Media and Technology Charter School in Boston. Using a basic script, Sposato makes approximately 100 calls per week to parents on his cell phone during his commute home every evening. Using the speed dial from the bank of contacts he has programmed into his phone, Sposato has developed a technique to communicate with parents in short messages and phone conversations. Sposato is proactively communicating with parents who are in his latent public and subtly encouraging them to move into the active public. At the same time, he is satisfying the parents' communication needs who are in his aware and active publics (Shorr, 2004). In slightly more than 3 hours per week, Sposato is able to personally communicate with parents, many of whom have probably never received a phone call from a principal before.

The cell phone should be used not only for outgoing phone calls but also for incoming phone calls. Just like a principal's e-mail address, the cell phone number should not be kept a secret. The number should be readily available on the Web site and business cards as well as any communication that comes directly from the principal, such as in letters and the e-mail signature and on the voice mail at the school as an immediate way to be reached.

Cell phones are not just cell phones anymore. Many are literally handheld computers. Even the Blackberry has many more options than just e-mail correspondence. Cell phones are also cameras, calendars, address books, walkie-talkies, and pagers, and they are used to access e-mail and the Internet. Text messaging is another feature that a principal should consider using. Similar to e-mail, text messaging and instant messaging are even more immediate and do not tie a principal to a desk. Text messaging is becoming more widespread to communicate with large groups of people simultaneously. For example, the Amber Alert system has implemented technology to reach the public not only through television, radio, and highway signs but also through text messaging on cell phones and handheld computers.

As with any other technology, cell phones have their benefits and their drawbacks. Lost calls, uncharged batteries, and weak signals are just a few. There is also the issue of the rules and regulations of cell phone usage in schools by teachers and students, which are different in every school district. Another issue concerns the use of cell phones during a crisis, which is discussed in greater detail in Chapter 9.

Even today, most principals are not supplied cell phones by the district, and many, understandably, are reluctant to give out their private cell phone numbers or even their home phone numbers. District-supplied cell phones for principals make sense. The demand on a principal's time continues to increase, and the expectation of constant communication also continues to rise. Using the techniques that are commonplace in the corporate world must become part of the principal's communication tool box.

As for e-mail, unique rules of etiquette are developing for cell phones. No principal would interrupt a parent conference in his or her office to take a phone call. Some of the same rules apply with cell phones. For example, when meeting with a community leader or a parent, cell phone calls should be forwarded to the school office or voice mail. Principals may choose to use the vibrate function when walking the school hallways. Also, principals should change voice mail messages frequently to include enough details so that those trying to communicate with principals know when they will be available.

Again, however, the cell phone is another tool and does not replace the landline. Technology has made even the traditional phone a better communication tool. What do callers to your school hear if they are put on hold? Elevator Muzak? Even the hold function can become a good communication tool for the school. A personal message from the principal could be recorded every Monday as a hold message and include upcoming events and general announcements about what is going on at the school.

Phone banks, although not new technology, represent a quick and active way to communicate for everyday reminders and sometimes in emergency situations. Essentially, voice broadcast systems, or automated phone calls alerting parents and key publics about snow closings, board or community meeting reminders, or even a school play, are proactive ways to communicate without having to make hundreds of phone calls. Instead, a personalized recorded message is heard. When the need arises to communicate with many but the content is the same, a phone bank can be an incredible time saver.

Keeping Up With Technology

Communication technologies are rapidly becoming more sophisticated, user-friendly, and available at reasonable prices. Handheld devices that include cell phones, voice mail, calendars, e-mail, digital photography and video recording, games, and Web access are some of the best-selling devices on the market today. Principals may not need a camera phone or even want to have a calendar function. What works best for one principal may not work well for another. For some, checking e-mail on handheld computers may be an efficient use of time. Other principals may feel comfortable with Tablet PCs that are easy to carry and used like a notepad. This is just a case of personal preference and comfort level with these products. Principals need to keep up with what is available, however, since stakeholders are using these devices. With these tools, it is not surprising to receive immediate replies to e-mails and voice mails from parents and partners. Even a PTA president could respond to a voice mail within seconds as she sits on a beach in the Caribbean on a family vacation.

Besides Web sites, e-mails, and cell phones, other technology options can be used. Fax blasts, although not as popular as they were several years ago, are yet another option. Computer software has revolutionized presentations, particularly Microsoft PowerPoint. Desktop publishing and color printers have changed the expectations for school programs. Although a principal may not need to be an expert desktop publisher, someone on the team should be able to use these tools. It is amazing to consider how many current students learned to surf the Web and play computer games long before they could even write their last name. The principal and the communications team will need to decide how many communication tools are manageable and how the audiences want to hear from the school. Thus, we return to how to communicate effectively and with what tool. The only way to know is to ask—on forms, written questionnaires, online, and in person.

With everyone always connected, a principal may start to feel the need to be "on" at all times, and some stakeholders may expect that. Unless it is a time of crisis, however, parents and others will not expect a principal to answer a call or e-mail at 2 a.m. It is important, however, that principals determine the best ways to reach their key stakeholders and realize that that medium is going to vary from regular phone calls placed to their offices or homes to calls made directly to their cell phones, calls on voice mail, notes sent to their e-mail systems at home or work, notes sent home with their children, and old-fashioned surface or "snail mail" sent through the U.S. Postal Service. The principal should also ensure that stakeholders know the principal's preferred method of receiving messages, and then the principal should act on them when he or she does receive messages.

To keep up with technology and how it is being used in schools, the Web site www.techlearning.com is a very good resource for principals.

Summary

The school Web site is becoming one of the most important communication tools for principals. As Internet usage continues to increase, the Web site should be viewed as a resource as well as an opening for positive two-way communication. A school Web site should include everything from the lunch menu to the crisis communication plan and a list of e-mail addresses of everyone in the school.

Technology has also introduced e-mail, cell phones, and instant messaging into a principal's communication tool box, making it faster and easier to deliver and respond to messages and concerns. Technology has also introduced some pitfalls, however, and basic communication techniques should not be abandoned.

9

Implementing Effective Communication Practices

This chapter examines effective communication techniques and tactics that are based on the broad base of communication theory reviewed previously. Generally, it is important that principals communicate with stakeholders in ways in which they feel most comfortable. Therefore, principals who are effective communicators learn to communicate through multiple channels.

The key question is three-pronged: (a) What communication tools are appropriate? (b) In which situation? and (c) With which key audience? Latent, aware, and active publics each require a different level of communication at different times, and that level is also dependent on the messages and issues. Latent publics rarely begin by looking for information; aware publics typically seek specific information to help form an opinion that will help them decide whether to move into an active communication mode. Updated information on the school's Web site that stakeholders can access easily, with the ability to send feedback and post inquiries, may be exactly the right forum and adequate communication for a principal's aware public the majority of the time. The active group requires more proactive communication. There are two kinds of active publics. One is a critical friend. The other is a critical enemy, or one that has already formed a negative opinion on the issue(s). Although principals should not ignore the critical "enemies," efforts should be focused on developing strong relationships and creating a group of active "friendly" Partners.

Essentially, a principal can build a support base by effectively communicating with the partnership of the school, parents, and community as discussed previously. In the end, this support base is part of a principal's communications team. Principals who are active communicators before issues become problems, before situations becomes crises, and before rumblings become rumors are likely to gain the support of active Enablers, Partners, and Friends and offset the vocal critical enemies. Proactive communication can also provide the principal with a buffer from the active publics that form around one single issue—for example, the neighbors who are concerned about new portable classrooms but otherwise have nothing to do with the school besides proximity.

As noted previously, it may seem that principals would want the latent publics to remain latent and the aware publics to remain aware so they can concentrate on their active publics. The question many principals may ask themselves is, Why would I want to stir up the latent publics when the aware and active publics already take up so much time? Some days that may make sense. Principals should also consider that a supportive, active public is also an asset. Actively communicating with the aware groups is to a principal's advantage. The aware public wants their principal to be a leader and to provide them with direction and advice. Encouraging aware audiences to become active audiences makes them feel involved. In fact, there may be several in the aware audience, and even the latent group, who principals will want to strongly encourage to become active. This does require effective communication from the school, however. A latent or aware public is not going to become active until they understand the issue or problem and believe that their involvement is necessary. Once involved, this could mean a stronger support base for the school when issues arise and in day-to-day operations: more parent volunteers, more support from community leaders, more active teachers and staff, and more Friends at the district office.

Thus, how does a principal effectively communicate with stakeholders?

The following are potential situations and possible communication tactics that principals can use with their Enablers, Partners, and Friends:

Situation: The calendar of events for the school year is released.

Stakeholder	Public	Type of Communication
Parents	Aware/active	Send home material, post on the Web site, e-mail
School staff	Active	Deliver to school mailboxes, e-mail
Reporter	Latent	Mail or fax, e-mail

The school calendar is a key tool that parents and staff rely on throughout the year. It is important that the calendar is readily available in a number of different mediums.

Situation: The principal needs to add six portable classrooms to her campus next year.

Stakeholder	Public	Type of Communication
School staff	Active	Face-to-face meeting, memos with updates
Parents/ students	Active	Memo with details, face-to-face meeting, updates on the Web site
Homeowners	Latent	Letter with explanation, schedule community meeting

In this situation, it is inevitable that staff, parents, and students will have concerns about portable classrooms that range from security to comfort. A principal who is proactive in communicating this situation will be taking the first step in alleviating concerns before they become critical issues.

Situation: A student at the school was awarded first place in a state essay contest.

Stakeholder	Public	Type of Communication
Student/ parents	Active	Note of congratulations, phone call home

Teachers	Aware	E-mail
All parents/ students	Latent	Newsletter, Web site

Personal notes and phone calls do not have to be time-consuming but are very good ways to acknowledge positive student accomplishments.

Situation: A well-known teacher becomes sick and suddenly dies.

Stakeholder	Public	Type of Communication
Students/ teachers	Active/ aware	Assembly/classroom meetings, information on grief counseling resources
Parents	Active/ aware	Memo home the same day, phone calls to active parents, follow-up memos and e-mails on grief counseling resources and arrangements
Family members	Active	Personal visit/phone call

Nobody wants to hear about a death over the loud speaker. Principals should take the time to visit teachers and students. In a large school, principals may have to enlist others, such as the assistant principal, to communicate this type of event in a timely manner.

Situation: A teacher spots a "possible" gun in a student's locker.

Stakeholder	Public	Type of Communication
District office	Active	Phone call immediately
Parents	Latent/aware/ active	Phone calls to parents with children directly involved in the incident, letter home that day, e-mail with additional information and resources
Media	Latent/ aware	Respond as soon as possible, refer to district office if necessary

Safety of students and staff should be the principal's first concern. Once everyone is safe, communication to key stakeholders is clear.

Principals Need a Communications Team

A principal's communications team needs to include members of the active publics—the Enablers, Partners, and Friends. Specifically, the central office and its staff, teachers and others in the school, as well as active parents and PTA board members are all people who can aid and enhance a principal's communication processes.

The central district office needs to be a part of the communications team. Whether the district has one public information officer or a team of seasoned professionals, the district should have resources to help principals communicate with the media, develop a Web site, and so on. It is worth a principal's time to develop and nurture these relationships by getting to know the key communicators and information technology staff as well as the district's policies governing their use. These resources can make a principal a more effective communicator (Box 9.1).

Teachers and staff play several key roles. Just as a CEO of a corporation relies on salespeople, managers, and employees to be on the front line with customers and consumers, in a school setting the assistant principal, teachers, office staff, and assistants are often the first and most frequent link to students, parents, and community members. Just as the principal may be asked to communicate information from the district level, a principal often relies on teachers and staff to communicate to parents and students. Therefore, it is important that a principal communicates frequently and honestly with the school's internal audience to ensure that everyone is well informed with correct information.

Internal communication in the corporate world is a discipline in itself. Entire departments focus on internal communication for several reasons. One is to garner support or, in other words, to ensure that there is buy-in from employees on the company's mission and vision, values, and programs. The other is to develop a single, unified voice that carries the organization's key messages consistently and accurately.

Empowering others to be communication aides does not mean that a principal will not continue to be the key communicator. It does not mean that a principal will lose control of communications coming from the school. What it does mean, however, is that key publics will hear a consistent message from several different voices, confirming and affirming the key message(s) the school needs to communicate.

Fortunately, those that surround most principals are probably excellent resources. Staff members, teachers, active parents, involved community members, and even students, especially in secondary schools, can be invaluable communication team members. Parents who are advertising executives by day can be an excellent marketing resource for principals the rest of the time they have available to counsel and advise on strategies. Public relations professionals can help principals outline and develop crisis communication plans. Web-savvy students may have the skills and talent to help run the school's Web site. A principal's team should include partners with skills in such jobs as

- Graphic designer
- Journalist
- Web master
- Event planner
- Marketing
- Public relations
- Fund raiser
- Volunteer coordinator

Box 9.1   The Basics of Effective Communication

- Be honest. Be direct.
- Talk with your publics, not to them.
- Be professional.
- Be a leader by listening. Take the time to listen.
- Remember who your publics are. Know them and their concerns.
- Be consistent. Be precise. Be clear with your message.
- Be compassionate. Show empathy.
- Be passionate. Emotion conveys caring.
- Share good news. Do not avoid bad news.
- Be visible. Be available. Be responsive.
- Elicit help. Let your Partners and critical Friends help you communicate with others.
- Be yourself.

For more on general communication techniques, see Ramsey (2002).

Principals Need to Be Communicating Constantly

This section focuses on the use of electronic communication tools, but some of the tried and true ways of communicating are still very effective. Principals and the communications team need to constantly communicate. The more communication, the more likely stakeholders will become involved in the school. Communicate with the parents—inform them of issues and get them involved and volunteering—and move them from latent to aware and active. Generally, if a group is informed and knowledgeable, it is more likely to be involved and more likely to pay attention to communication from the school.

How does a principal do that? The trick is to develop many activities and events to encourage involvement. Principals should pack the school calendar with as many events as possible with the goal of getting the parents, as well as other key stakeholders, to the school. Although parents seem like the most obvious public for events, local politicians, business leaders, and even the media are aware of and should be invited to events. The PTA/PTO is an excellent group to tap into and to coordinate events with the school. The events should be publicized with a streaming flow of communication—fliers, brochures, bulletins, and calendars. This is an opportunity for principals to be creative with events that bring key stakeholders to the school on evenings and weekends. Holding events during the day may be fine for some stay-at-home parents, but principals should be cognizant of all the stakeholders' busy schedules.

Other ways to get stakeholders into the school include activities such as parent workshops on topics ranging from health issues to parenting and homework help. A secure parent room or parent center where parents can pick up and drop off their children, as well as meet each other, has proven to be successful in a number of schools.

The school newsletter to parents is probably one of the most important communication tools and an essential element of a principal's communication plan. Principals need to find a way to produce at a minimum one per month, and in addition to the printed version, the newsletter should be available on the Web site and distributed broadly to stakeholders via e-mail. Successful communication through the newsletter is based on several factors: consistency in delivery, clarity of articles, and timeliness of content.

The newsletter needs to be a tool that parents and others, including teachers and students, rely on to arrive the same time each month or each week. For example, one kindergarten teacher sends home a "what's happening this week" every Monday afternoon to keep parents up-to-date on not only the academic focus of the week but also special events. Principals can also find the time to do a weekly newsletter (see Chapter 5).

School Newsletter Articles Need to Be Short

Principals should keep in mind how many stakeholders are reading the newsletter. Parents are probably glancing through them while making dinner. Students may be just scanning them on the school bus. Teachers may add it to a stack of papers to grade and be happy just to get to it in the next couple of days. Therefore, headlines need to be straightforward and clear. The articles need to be short, with the key points in short sentences, "active language," and without educational jargon. Principals should also make the newsletter a piece that everyone wants to save. It would be helpful if it contained an easy-to-read calendar that could be pinned on a corkboard or stuck to the refrigerator so it could be referenced at a glance.

The following are additional tips on how to develop an effective newsletter:

1. Be informative. A school newsletter's main purpose should be to inform parents, students, and staff on items that they need and want to hear about.

2. Be succinct. Understand how busy the parents are, and make it easy to scan the newsletter for items of particular interest. Also, make sure the copy is filled with the most pertinent information easy to find.

3. Answer frequently asked questions. Is the school secretary finding that callers are asking the same series of questions? Respond to these questions in the newsletter.

4. Keep design accessible and inviting.

5. Engage readers. Ask for contributions. Request feedback—written or via e-mail, the Web site, or phone.

6. Provide more information. Give them the Web site and other addresses to go for more information.

For all principals, there should never be a shortage of topics to be included in the newsletter, including highlights of all the good things going on at the school. The newsletter should also include a principal's column.

Carolyn Warner, a veteran educator and communicator, offers some additional thoughts on content in her book *Promoting Your School* (2000, pp. 51–52):

- Introduce various curriculum programs.
- Highlight student achievements.
- Review rules and regulations that are of specific concern.
- Provide homework tips for parents and students.
- Add suggested reading lists.
- List additional resources that are available to parents in the community.
- Summarize test results and provide information on where full reports are available.
- Profile a staff member, or ask him or her to write a "guest" column.
- Provide updates and summaries from PTA, board, and other meetings.
- Include district news.
- Solicit volunteers.

Warner also suggests that principals may want to produce several newsletters: one for each major stakeholder group—a parent newsletter and a teacher and staff newsletter—and one for the community and local businesses. This sounds like a great idea, but there are always time and manpower issues. Therefore, perfect the parent newsletter before moving on to additional publications.

Sending Messages Home Should Be Routine

Sending mailers and letters, as well as flyers, brochures, and personal notes, home with the kids should also be routine. Remember the old advertising adage: When first exposed to a message, the receiver may only take a minimal notice. At second exposure, the audience may pay more attention. It is only the third or fourth time a message is sent that the audience may decide if they really need to take action. Although certain issues may pique the interest of key publics the first time, with topics such as the need for volunteers, openings on the PTA board, and an upcoming fund-raiser, the three-rule minimum does apply.

For example, when a principal is preparing for a parent volunteer orientation, the meeting announcement should be sent home, posted on the Web site, noted on the principal's voice mail and "hold" feature, and added to the school's outdoor message sign at least 1 week prior to the meeting. Through these four different communication mediums, the principal will reach target publics probably two or three times, increasing the likelihood that they received the message, thought about it, and will attend.

Last are handbooks, which should be available in both a printed and an electronic format. At one time, a school handbook included only attendance policies, discipline and code of conduct policies, and dress code guidelines. These are still pertinent topics and need to be included. Emergency preparedness and guidelines are essential, however, and may even deserve their own handbook, as well as a special back-to-school meeting. As explored in Chapters 5 and 6, crises and emergencies pose a unique set of communication issues. It is important not only for the principal to be prepared but also for the teachers, staff, parents, students, and other stakeholders to have a guide before a crisis occurs.

As with all other tactics and techniques, there are pitfalls. The world of desktop publishing and color printers has created a whole host of problems. First, desktop publishing has given the most inartistic the ability to "design." Parents do not expect the newsletter to be professionally designed. What they do expect is an easy-to-read calendar and short notes on important issues. Color printers have provided the ability to use pink and purple in headlines. Color can be a wonderful tool. For the school's communication, keep it simple and professional. Inexpensive clip art makes it easy to add many graphics to even the most straightforward announcements. There is no need for a graphic to be included with every newsletter article and no need for more than one or two on a school program or announcement.

Principals should examine the newsletter and other forms of printed communications. One common mistake is the use of many fonts. Another issue with fonts is the difference between serif and sans serif. Most books are printed with a serif font such as Times or Garamond. Online, in e-mails and on Web sites, sans serif fonts such as Arial and Veranda are used. Generally, the rule of thumb is serif fonts in printed materials and san serif fonts online. White space or plenty of room on the page is good. Crowding a page with too many things makes it difficult to read. Principals should collect good brochures and fliers from other organizations and borrow some of the best design ideas for school communications.

In general, the principal's communication team should include an art/graphics or journalism teacher or both. These people are an excellent addition to the team, as are other Partners who have experience in graphics and writing.

Consistency is also important. The school needs to use a masthead that has the school's name or logo or both, address and phone number, and Web site and that is used every time the newsletter is published. The newsletter is just one of the principal's tools that supplement every other communication effort.

Principals Increasingly Are Marketing Their Schools

Although an extensive review of the body of advertising and marketing research is not necessary here, as noted previously, some of the basic principles do underscore the conclusions of the public relations research discussed in Part I and support the "do's" and "don'ts" of traditional communication tactics. Specifically, the concept of branding is something for a principal to keep in mind. In brief, branding is the promise school principals keep to their publics. Whether it is well developed or not, each school has a brand, or more simply an image, in the minds of its stakeholders. Although principals may not be facing the same competitive issues as companies who market consumer products, branding is making its way into education through colleges and universities as well as private primary and secondary schools. In fact, many private schools and local teachers' associations retain a marketing and advertising agency as well as a public relations agency. Principals should take close notice of advertisements in the newspaper, and even radio commercials, for local private schools. What is their message? What is their brand?

What is the branding lesson for public school principals?

- Consistency: Consistency in message(s); consistency in the look and feel of the printed and electronic communications; consistency among the many voices from the school.
- Dynamics: The need to set the school apart from others.
- Emotion: An appeal to the publics' emotions. Emotion sells coffee, lipstick, and shoes. The same appeal works for support for the school.

Of course, there is the old-fashioned face-to-face communication that has not gone out of style. Parents and other partners appreciate principals who take the time to shake hands at back-to-school night, greet parents at the second-grade holiday musical, and watch the football game in the bleachers. Also, principals should not take general visibility in and around the school for granted.

Being visible does not have to be too time-consuming for principals. Even small gestures, such as standing outside the school's front doors as parents drop off their kids, can make a major impression. Creative visibility solutions include shopping at the neighborhood grocery store, even if the principal does not live in the immediate area.

In addition, the practice of home visits is making a comeback in some areas (Mathews, 2005, p. A07). Whether it is visiting struggling students or new students or making an effort to visit every student's home, the consensus seems to be that a principal's home visit encourages parental involvement and opens up a positive dialogue between the school leader and the family.

Meeting community leaders and developing a relationship with them may prove to be more difficult for principals, and it is probably not their highest priority. If principals have the energy and the time, however, it is best to meet these leaders where they feel most comfortable—at chamber of commerce meetings and mixers. This face-to-face communication will test a principal's networking skills, but it is another way to get out into the community and give others the opportunity to provide feedback.

In addition, for all stakeholders—from latent to active—the school sign outside the school is a prominent communication tool. This sign should be used to its fullest potential by keeping the information current, announcing events and school holidays, and providing friendly messages, such as congratulating the school's top scholars.

For more tips on communication and marketing schools, see Warner (2000).

Good News Will Attract the Media

Communicating with the media requires a unique set of skills, patience and persistence, and is a topic of entire textbooks and handbooks. With so much else to do, media communications is probably not a priority for most principals. Generally, if there are good things happening in the school, the news will reach the media. It is important that principals be prepared to deal with the media during a crisis, which was discussed previously. This discussion provides some general tips and thoughts on basic media relations.

Press releases, news articles, and feature stories are excellent ways to communicate with the school's stakeholders. The newspaper is a communication medium in which a principal cannot control what is written, however. This is just one of the many reasons why developing a relationship with the communications staff at the district level, and getting to know the education reporters in the region, is so critical.

Before embarking on a media blitz, principals should have a public information officer from the district office as a partner, even if the principal will be communicating directly with the media for both good and bad news. In addition, working with the media is an excellent opportunity to include the school's PTA/PTO. Many PTA/PTOs have communications or public relations committees that are tasked with the duty of promoting the positive things going on at the school.

If there is no such committee in place, a principal should help them form one with parent volunteers and, ultimately, new members of the principal's communication team. Parents like to see positive stories about their school, and those with the education and talent are usually more than willing to help. Principals should let this committee be proactive with good news. One of the major complaints of reporters and editors is the timeliness of story ideas. Something that happened 1 week ago is not news. If the school has good news, or an upcoming event (not a past event) announcement, the committee should let the media know as soon as possible. Particularly in smaller communities, school stories are popular. Local papers like photographs, and parents and kids like to see themselves in the paper, including names listed for honor role, clubs, and sport teams. Has the PTA/PTO or school made the investment in a digital camera? Having one on hand, with consent forms, will help the PTA/PTO get good news out and make you the reporter's friend. In addition, make it a habit in your office for key reporters and editors to receive your event calendars. Principals are of course thrilled when a good story runs. When a bad news story runs, however, unless there are factual errors, complaining to a writer or editor does not help. In addition, responding to every editorial may not be necessary, but it should at least be considered. Principals should consider whether a response from a PTA/PTO president or a parent partner may be more effective.

The very basics of dealing with reporters are as follows:

- Be proactive and timely with good news.
- Be responsive with bad news.
- Be honest.
- Respond as quickly as possible.

If you do not know an answer, say so. Do not say, "No comment." Find out the accurate information, and call the reporter back.

Respect reporters' deadlines. Radio, television, and newspaper reporters all work on different deadlines, but all deadlines are typically tight and hectic.

One of the major benefits for principals and schools that develop a cordial relationship with local reporters is that when a crisis does occur, they already understand the school, its staff, and its partners.

For more tips and tactics on dealing with the media, refer to *Good News: How to Get the Best Possible Media Coverage for Your School*, by Gail Conners (2000).

Summary

This chapter addressed the basics of effective communication tactics. By focusing on communication efforts with partners, building a strong communications team, tapping into districtwide resources, and utilizing myriad tools, principals can be effective communicators.

Generally, an effective communicator uses many different tactics and techniques. Newsletters, fliers, and calendars are still appropriate ways to communicate with parents, students, and all partners. The media are also an outlet that a principal needs to be cognizant of and be prepared to respond to; a principal will be better served communicating directly with the school's Partners, however, and should rely on the district's communication team and the PTA/PTO for media relations support.

10

Answering the Call to Leadership

Not long ago, the education interest groups in Washington, D.C., were at their wits' end trying to get Congress to focus on the needs of the public schools. It seemed impossible. After the "Great Society" and civil rights legislation of the mid-1960s, other issues intruded onto the scene, and education moved to the back burner. There was no Department of Education to command the spotlight. Rather, there was an "E" stuck uncomfortably between an "H" and a "W" in the Department of Health, Education, and Welfare, and the two bookend agencies made up most of the behemoth's bulk and used all its resources. The Office of Education got the leftovers from the congressional appropriation committees that considered the department's annual funding. Even those who lobbied for education were outnumbered and outclassed by their counterparts from health and welfare. Education interest groups would lament that what the country needed was another Sputnik. Then they got their wish. It was not the creation of the Department of Education. That did not do much more than rearrange offices within the federal bureaucracy. What made the difference was the release of the Nation at Risk report. It went off like a rocket from Washington, D.C., and awoke America to what was supposedly a crisis in public education. Life as a school administrator has not been the same since.

Policy Board Develops Administrator Standards

The federal focus brought much attention to the role of the school principal. One consequence was pressure from policymakers and others to provide higher-quality leadership in the public schools. This inevitably led to a question about the standards being used to admit applicants into the profession and to ensure their quality once on the job. Most states required new principals to be certified or licensed before going into school administration. The standards varied greatly from one state to another, however. Consequently, in the early 1990s the states formed a consortium to develop a common set of standards.

At the same time, the National Policy Board for Educational Administration, consisting of the 10 national associations most concerned about school administrators,[1] decided to create standards by which to judge the worth of their profession. The policy board teamed up with the Interstate School Leaders Licensure Consortium (ISLLC) and produced the *Standards for School Leaders* (ISLLC, 1996). These standards are used today by most state departments of education when considering applicants for administrator licensure. The policy board also used the *Standards for School Leaders* as the basis for developing *Standards for Advanced Programs in Educational Leadership*, the criteria by which departments of educational administration qualify to be designated "nationally recognized" when applying for certification by the National Council for the Accreditation of Teacher Education (NCATE) (www.npbea.org).

Undergirding the ISLLC standards is an understanding that the principal is going to be a master at communication management. Each of the six standards describes "performances" that an administrator facilitates and engages in. Consider the following six ISLLC (1996) standards and how each of them specifically touches on communication management. Readers should consider the extent to which they now are able to master many of the performance requirements necessary to satisfy the ISLLC standards.

Standard 1: A school administrator is an educational leader who promotes the success of all students by facilitating the development, articulation, implementation, and stewardship of a vision of learning that is shared and supported by the school community.

The administrator facilitates processes and engages in activities ensuring that

- the vision and mission of the school are effectively communicated to staff, parents, students, and community members;
- the vision and mission are communicated through the use of symbols, ceremonies, stories, and similar activities;
- the core beliefs of the school vision are modeled for all stakeholders;
- the contributions of school community members to the realization of the vision are communicated to all stakeholders;
- an implementation plan is developed in which objectives and strategies to achieve the vision and goals are clearly articulated;
- assessment data related to student learning are used to develop the school vision and goals;
- barriers to achieving the vision are identified, clarified, and addressed; and
- the vision, mission, and implementation plans are regularly monitored, evaluated, and revised.

Standard 2: A school administrator is an educational leader who promotes the success of all students by advocating, nurturing, and sustaining a school culture and instructional program conducive to student learning and staff professional growth.

The administrator facilitates processes and engages in activities ensuring that

- a variety of sources of information are used to make decisions;
- multiple sources of information regarding performance are used by staff and students; and
- pupil personnel programs are developed to meet the needs of students and their families.

Standard 3: A school administrator is an educational leader who promotes the success of all students by ensuring management of the organization, operations, and resources for a safe, efficient, and effective learning environment.

The administrator facilitates and engages in activities ensuring that

- problems are confronted and resolved in a timely manner;
- the school acts entrepreneurially to support continuous improvement;
- stakeholders are involved in decisions affecting schools;

- responsibility is shared to maximize ownership and accountability;
- effective communication skills are used; and
- there is effective use of technology to manage school operations.

Standard 4: A school administrator is an educational leader who promotes the success of all students by collaborating with families and community members, responding to diverse community interests and needs, and mobilizing community resources.

The administrator facilitates and engages in activities ensuring that

- high visibility, active involvement, and communication with the larger community are a priority;
- relationships with community leaders are identified and nurtured;
- information about family and community concerns, expectations, and needs is used regularly;
- there is outreach to different business, religious, political, and service agencies and organizations;
- credence is given to individuals and groups whose values and opinions may conflict;
- the school and community serve one another as resources;
- available community resources are secured to help the school solve problems and achieve goals;
- partnerships are established with area businesses, institutions of higher education, and community groups to strengthen programs and support school goals;
- community youth family services are integrated with school programs;
- community stakeholders are treated equitably;
- diversity is recognized and valued;
- effective media relations are developed and maintained;
- a comprehensive program of community relations is established; and
- community collaboration is modeled for staff.

Standard 5: A school administrator is an educational leader who promotes the success of all students by acting with integrity, fairness, and in an ethical manner.

The administrator

- demonstrates a personal and professional code of ethics;
- demonstrates values, beliefs, and attitudes that inspire others to higher levels of performance;
- serves as a role model;
- treats people fairly, equitable, and with dignity and respect;
- protects the rights and confidentiality of students and staff;
- demonstrates appreciation for and sensitivity to the diversity in the school community;
- recognizes and respects the legitimate authority of others;
- examines and considers the prevailing values of the diverse school community;
- opens the school to public scrutiny; and
- applies laws and procedures fairly, wisely, and considerably.

Standard 6: A school administrator is an education leader who promotes the success of all students by understanding, responding to, and influencing the larger political, social, economical, legal, and cultural context.

The administrator facilitates and engages in activities ensuring that

- the environment in which schools operate is influenced on behalf of students and their families;
- communication occurs among the school community concerning trends, issues, and potential changes in the environment in which schools operate;
- there is ongoing dialogue with representatives of diverse community groups; and
- lines of communication are developed with decision makers outside the school community.

With Standards Comes Excellence

Nearly every state department of education has adopted the ISLLC standards or incorporated them into their licensure requirements. Furthermore, the ISLLC standards form the backbone of the criteria that NCATE uses when it reviews departments of educational administration. Therefore, the vast majority of university-based administrator preparation programs throughout the country now feature the ISLLC performance standards, which means that readers who have finished this book will be better prepared than most to answer the call to assume a leadership post in one of the nation's public schools.

Laurel Schmidt (2002) reminds her fellow principals that no matter how much they do or how well they do it, they are going to be criticized. She says, "There's no escaping it—if you choose to be a principal, the minefield is not optional" (p. xii). Principals who become masters at communication management are not going to avoid the minefield, but they are more likely to know how to make their way through it successfully.

Your stakeholders await your leadership.

Note

1. American Association of Colleges for Teacher Education, American Association of School Administrators, Association for Supervision and Curriculum Development, Council of Chief State School Officers, National Association of Elementary School Principals, National Association of Secondary School Principals, National Council for Accreditation of Teacher Education, National Council of Professors of Educational Administration, National School Boards Association, and University Council for Educational Administration.

References

Aldrich, H., & Herker, D. (1977). Boundary spanning roles and organization structure. *Academy of Management Review, 2,* 217–230.

Archer, J. (2005, February 16). R.I. state commissioner imposes plan of action on Providence school. *Education Week,* p. 9.

Bacharach, S. B., & Mundell, B. (Eds.). (1995). *Images of schools: Structures and roles in organizational behavior.* Thousand Oaks, CA: Corwin.

Bagin, D., & Gallagher, D. R. (2001). *The school and community relations.* Boston: Allyn & Bacon.

Bernays, E. L. (1952). *Public relations.* Norman: University of Oklahoma Press.

Bracey, G. W. (2000). *Bail me out: Handling difficult data and tough questions about public schools.* Thousand Oaks, CA: Corwin.

Buchanan, B. (1974). Building organizational commitment: The socialization of managers in work organizations. *Administrative Science Quarterly, 19,* 533–546.

Carroll, A. B. (1989). *Business & society: Ethics and stakeholder management.* Cincinnati, OH: South-Western.

Conners, G. A. (2000). *Good news: How to get the best possible media coverage for your school.* Thousand Oaks, CA: Corwin.

Cutlip, S. M., & Center, A. H. (1958). *Effective public relations* (2nd ed.). Englewood Cliffs, NJ: Prentice Hall.

Dozier, D. M. (with Grunig, L. A., & Grunig, J. E.). (1995). *Manager's guide to excellence in public relations and communication management.* Mahwah, NJ: Lawrence Erlbaum.

Epstein, J. L. (1992). School and family partnerships. In M. Alkin (Ed.), *Encyclopedia of educational research* (6th ed., pp. 1139–1151). New York: Macmillan.

Epstein, J. L. (2001). *School, family, and community partnerships: Preparing educators and improving schools.* Boulder, CO: Westview.

Epstein, J. L. (2002a). School, family, and community partnerships: Caring for the children we share. In J. L. Epstein, M. G. Sanders, B. S. Simon, K. C. Salinas, N. R. Jansorn, & F. L. Voorhis (Eds.), *School, family, and community partnerships: Your handbook for action* (2nd ed.). Thousand Oaks, CA: Corwin.

Epstein, J. L. (2002b). Improving school, family, and community partnerships in middle and high schools. In J. L. Epstein, M. G. Sanders, B. S. Simon, K. C. Salinas, N. R. Jansorn, & F. L. Voorhis (Eds.), *School, family, and community partnerships: Your handbook for action* (2nd ed.). Thousand Oaks, CA: Corwin.

Epstein, J. L., & Connors, L. J. (1995). School and family partnerships in the middle grades. In B. Rutherford (Ed.), *Creating family-school partnerships* (pp. 137–166). Columbus, OH: National Middle School Association.

Epstein, J. L., & Sanders, M. G. (2000). School, family, and community connections: New directions for social research. In M. Hallinan (Ed.), *Handbook of sociology of education* (pp. 285–306). New York: Plenum.

Epstein, J. L., Sanders, M. G., Simon, B. S., Salinas, K. C., Jansorn, N. R., and Van Voorhis, F. L. (Eds.). (2002). *School, family, and community partnerships: Your handbook for action* (2nd ed.). Thousand Oaks, CA: Corwin.

Epstein, N. (Ed.). (2004). *Who's in charge here: The tangled web of school governance and policy.* Denver, CO: Education Commission of the States.

Farkus, S., Foley, P., & Duffett, A. (2001). *Just waiting to be asked: A fresh look at attitudes on public engagement.* New York: Public Agenda.

Freeman, R. E. (1984). *Strategic management: A stakeholder approach.* Boston: Pitman.

Goodwin, R. H. (2004, August). A summary of the findings of the 2003 NCPEA Morphet Award Dissertation. *NCPEA Education Leadership Review, 5,* 16–19.

Grunig, J. E. (1989). Symmetrical presuppositions as a framework for public relations theory. In C. H. Boltan & V. Hazelton (Eds.), *Public relations theory.* Hillsdale, NJ: Lawrence Erlbaum.

Grunig, J. E. (1997). A situational theory of publics: Conceptual history, recent challenges, and new research. In D. Moss, T. MacManus, & D. Vercic (Eds.). *Public relations research: An international perspective,* pp. 3-48. London: International Thomson Business Press.

Grunig, J. E. (Ed.) (with Dozier, D. M., Ehling, W. P., Grunig, L. A., Repper, F. C., & White, J.). (1992). *Excellence in public relations and communication management.* Hillsdale, NJ: Lawrence Erlbaum.

Grunig, J. E., & Grunig, L. A. (1989). Toward a theory of the public relations behavior of organizations. In J. E. Grunig and L. A. Grunig (Eds.), *Public relations research annual* (Vol. 1, pp. 27–63). Hillsdale, NJ: Lawrence Erlbaum.

Grunig, J. E., & Hunt, T. (1984). *Managing public relations.* New York: Holt, Rinehart & Winston.

Hart, A. W. (1995). Reconceiving school leadership: Emergent views. *Elementary School Journal, 96,* 9–28.

Henry, S. (2004, August 26). Venture capital's transparency trouble. *The Washington Post,* pp. E1, E6.

Hill, J. W. (1963). *The making of a public relations man.* New York: David McKay.

Interstate School Leaders Licensure Consortium. (1996). *Standards for school leaders*. Washington, DC: Council of Chief State School Officers.

Jemison, D. B. (1984). The importance of boundary spanning roles in strategic decision making. *Journal of Management Studies, 21,* 132–152.

Jones, G. R. (1983). Transaction costs, property rights, and organizational culture: An exchange perspective. *Administrative Science Quarterly, 28,* 454–467.

Mathematica Policy Research. (2004, June 9). *Teach for America teachers outperform novice and veteran colleagues in math; Achieve same results in reading as their peers, national study reveals.* Retrieved from http://www.mathematica.org

Mathews, J. (2004, July 13). When good isn't good enough. *The Washington Post.* Retrieved from http://www.washingtonpost.com

Mathews, J. (2005, March 8). Opening dialogue with a knock on the door. *The Washington Post,* p. A7.

Murphy, J. (1990). Principal instructional leadership. In L. S. Lotto & P. W. Thurston (Eds.), *Advances in educational administration: Changing perspectives on the school.* Greenwich, CT: JAI.

Murphy, J. (1999, April). *The quest for a center: Notes on the state of the profession of educational leadership.* Invited address, American Educational Research Association, Montreal.

Murphy, P. (1991). The limits of symmetry: A game theory approach to symmetric and asymmetric public relations. In L. A. Grunig and J. E. Grunig (Eds.), *Public relations research annual* (Vol. 3, pp. 115–132). Hillsdale, NJ: Lawrence Erlbaum.

National Policy Board for Educational Administration. (2002). *Standards for advanced programs in educational leadership.* Retrieved from http://www.npbea.org/program

National School Public Relations Association. (2001). *The complete crisis communication management manual.* Rockville, MD: Author.

National School Public Relations Association. (2004, August). Going from sour grapes to fine wine: Cultivating your grapevine to deliver a rich vintage. *Communication Matters for Leading Superintendents, 1*(3), 1.

Ramsey, R. D. (2002). *How to say the right thing every time: Communicating well with students, staff, parents and the public.* Thousand Oaks, CA: Corwin.

Ravitch, D. (2005, March 15). Failing the wrong grades. *New York Times,* p. 25.

Sanders, M. G. (2002). Community involvement in school improvement: The little extra that makes a big difference. In J. L. Epstein, M. G. Sanders, B. S. Simon, K. C. Salinas, N. R. Jansorn, & F. L. Voorhis (Eds.), *School, family, and community partnerships: Your handbook for action* (2nd ed.). Thousand Oaks, CA: Corwin.

Schmidt, L. (2002). *Gardening in the minefield: A survival guide for school administrators.* Portsmouth, NH: Heinemann.

Shedlin, A., Jr. (2004, January/February). Is your school father-friendly? *Principal, 83*(3), 22–25.

Shorr, P. W. (June 2004). *One call at a time.* Retrieved from http://www.scholastic.com/administrator/June.04/articles.asp?article=spotlight

Simon, B. S. (2002). Predictors and effects of family involvement in high school. In J. L. Epstein, M. G. Sanders, B. S. Simon, K. C. Salinas, N. R. Jansorn, & F. L. Voorhis (Eds.), *School, family, and community partnerships: Your handbook for action,* pp. 235–245 (2nd ed.). Thousand Oaks, CA: Corwin.

Symylie, M. A., & Hart, A. W. (1999). School leadership for teacher learning and change: A human and social capital development perspective. In J. Murphy & K. S. Lewis (Eds.), *Handbook of research on educational administration* (2nd ed.). San Francisco: Jossey-Bass.

Teach for America. (2004, June). *Independent study shows Teach for America impact on student achievement.* Retrieved from http://www.teachfor america.org

Warner, C. (2000). *Promoting your school: Going beyond PR.* Thousand Oaks, CA: Corwin.

White, J., & Dozier, D. M. (1992). Public relations and management decision making. In J. E. Grunig (Ed.), *Excellence in public relations and communication management.* Hillsdale, NJ: Lawrence Erlbaum.

Wolcott, H. (1973). *The man in the principal's office: An ethnographic study.* New York: Holt, Rinehart & Winston.

Yukl, G. (1994). *Leadership in organizations* (3rd ed.). Englewood Cliffs, NJ: Prentice Hall.

Index

**CORWIN
PRESS**

The Corwin Press logo—a raven striding across an open book—represents the union of courage and learning. Corwin Press is committed to improving education for all learners by publishing books and other professional development resources for those serving the field of PreK–12 education. By providing practical, hands-on materials, Corwin Press continues to carry out the promise of its motto: **"Helping Educators Do Their Work Better."**

A co-publication with the American Association of School Administrators, the Leadership for Learning series is centered on student learning and is aligned with the Interstate School Leaders Licensure Consortium (ISLLC) and National Policy Board for Educational Administration (NPBEA) standards. Authored by leading experts, the series addresses the knowledge and capabilities that have been identified as essential for effective leadership in schools. Each volume in the series blends research, theory, and lessons from practice to help principals and other educational leaders solve the most critical challenges facing their schools. At a time when educators must implement research-based solutions to critical problems, this series is an important step towards keeping improved student achievement at the center of any accountability effort.